PRAISE FOR THE WORK OF DAVID DEIDA

"David Deida explains the heart and soul of a woman to men. As a woman, I've never felt so understood and validated. David's work is a key to helping men and women take their relationships one step further. Finally, a clear and brilliant guide to unraveling the mystery of relationships."

MARCI SHIMOFF Co-author of *Chicken Soup for the Woman's Soul*

"David Deida's teachings on this central human concern, sexuality, emanate from a deeply trustworthy source. He has undergone his own rigorous training and practice, which manifests in precise, gentle, and thorough teachings. Many spiritual traditions, including Zen, have excluded or marginalized the sexual experience. David's work fills this gap, and gives us a mature approach for bringing the energetic, emotional, and physical experience of sex into our life and practice. And like Zen, the fruition of David's work is openness, compassion, and love."

GENPO ROSHI Author of *Th- - - Sleeps*

"Every once in awhile, someone co-- next step. Their ideas seem to ans in the culture. Their books and se nd within a period of time their id vernacular. David Deida is such a person. In off from now, his ideas will have spread like wildfire."

MARIANNE WILLIAMSON Author of *A Return to Love*

"There are few categories I know of for an original like David; for his teachings there is no pigeonhole. He is a bridge-builder between East and West, between ancient and modern wisdom traditions regarding this least understood of all spiritual teachings: the mystery of intimacy as a yoga of transformation, transcendence, and self-realization. David Deida is the one Western teacher of tantra whose books I read and whom I send students to learn from. The results of true practice, in any tradition, are unmistakable; David Deida demonstrates them."

LAMA SURYA DAS Author of *Awakening the Buddha Within*

THE

Enlightened Sex

MANUAL

ALSO BY DAVID DEIDA

BOOKS

The Way of the Superior Man
*A Spiritual Guide to Mastering the Challenges of
Women, Work, and Sexual Desire*

Dear Lover
A Woman's Guide to Men, Sex, and Love's Deepest Bliss

Blue Truth
A Spiritual Guide to Life & Death and Love & Sex

Intimate Communion
Awakening Your Sexual Essence

Finding God Through Sex
Awakening the One of Spirit Through the Two of Flesh

Wild Nights
*Conversations with Mykonos about Passionate Love,
Extraordinary Sex, and How to Open to God*

Instant Enlightenment
Fast, Deep, and Sexy

It's a Guy Thing
An Owner's Manual for Women

AUDIO

Enlightened Sex
Finding Freedom & Fullness Through Sexual Union

The Teaching Sessions: The Way of the Superior Man
*Revolutionary Tools and Essential Exercises for Mastering the
Challenges of Women, Work, and Sexual Desire*

WEBSITE

www.deida.info

DAVID DEIDA

THE
Enlightened Sex
MANUAL

Sexual Skills for the Superior Lover

SOUNDS TRUE
Boulder, Colorado

Sounds True, Inc., Boulder, CO 80306

© 2004, 2007 David Deida

SOUNDS TRUE is a trademark of Sounds True, Inc.

Published 2007
Printed in Canada

ISBN 13: 978-1-59179-585-8

Library of Congress Cataloging-in-Publication Data

Deida, David.
  The enlightened sex manual : sexual skills for the superior lover / David
Deida.
    p. cm.
  Originally published in 2004.
  ISBN 978-1-59179-585-8 (pbk.)
  1. Sex instruction. I. Title.

HQ31D4125 2007
613.9'6—dc22

                                    2007019322

IMPORTANT CAUTION

Please read this

Although anyone may find the practices, disciplines, and understandings in this book to be useful, it is made available with the understanding that neither the author nor the publisher is engaged in presenting specific medical, psychological, emotional, sexual, or spiritual advice. Nor is anything in this book intended to be a diagnosis, prescription, recommendation, or cure for any specific kind of medical, psychological, emotional, sexual, or spiritual problem. Each person has unique needs, and this book cannot take these individual differences into account. Each person should engage in a program of treatment, prevention, cure, or general health only in consultation with a licensed, qualified physician, therapist, or other competent professional. Any person suffering from venereal disease or any local illness of his or her sexual organs or prostate gland should consult a medical doctor and a qualified instructor of sexual yoga before practicing the sexual methods described in this book.

CONTENTS

INTRODUCTION

Good artists are skilled, but *great* artists convey an immense depth of feeling through their expertise. The same goes for the art of sex. A good lover knows how to make the body sing. But a great lover, a *superior* lover, evokes a vast choir of bliss.

A good orgasm is satisfying, but a great orgasm can be a revelation of your deepest being, unfolding the bright truth of who you are in ecstatic communion with your lover. Sex can be a way of magnifying love's light through every cell, shining beyond fear, melding your hearts in the infinite radiance of being. Sex can be *enlightened*—or not.

Most of us bring our problems to bed with us: the tension from a stressful day, our past history of sexual failure, our need to be reassured that we are loved. As we bring light to every aspect of our sexuality, these kinds of difficulties are used to reflect our next place of opening, physically, emotionally, and spiritually. Every quandary is illuminated and unfolded by love's radiant presence. Every tussle is seen with wide-open eyes, embraced, accepted, and understood to be a potential doorway to the true desires of our soul.

The Enlightened Sex Manual shows how to transform the often willy-nilly flow of stimulated genital energy into a profound depth of feeling, openness, and embodied ecstasy. Sexual energy can fill your body with light, blow your mind with bliss, and melt all difference in an endless love that radiates as one heart.

When sexual energy emanates from its spiritual source, your cells are enlivened and your spirit rejuvenated by the same force that might otherwise have been thrown off in more trivial shivers and shakes. When you meld sexual intensity with open-hearted depth, your bliss grows spontaneously, fertilized by the forces of your fears, hopes, and anxieties.

You can allow the light of your soul to shine through the sexual play of your body, as long as you know how to deal with the habits that would otherwise prevent your enlightened loving. The practices presented in this book allow you to develop your sexual skills as gifts of spiritual rapture.

Part One describes how to circulate your internal energy so deep relaxation, delightful sensuality, and open-hearted loving can infuse your lovemaking with joy. Part Two focuses on ways for men and women to enjoy multiple, whole-body orgasms that serve as remembrances of your deepest and most effortless bliss of being. Part Three presents a range of techniques to enhance the fullness of sexual pleasure and spiritual openness. Part Four offers more advanced practices for those readers who wish to continue growing in their sexual capacities.

The practices in this book are presented for all partners in all relationships: men and women, gay and straight. At times, we will talk in terms of "masculine energy" and "feminine energy," which partners of either sex can choose to offer—perhaps even taking turns—to work with the polarities of attraction in both same-sex and opposite-sex relationships. At other times, we will illustrate specific techniques using examples that involve a man and a woman. But as you read, you will be able to experiment, modify, and apply the practices to your own sexual situation, while walking your unique path as a superior lover.

Part One:
Energy

Love's light seeks expression through our bodies, one way or another. But our sexual gift of deepest love is sometimes limited by a more superficial part of us: our emotional resistance, our fear of opening as the deep love that is our true nature.

We resist opening without limits because our superficial self wants to feel itself as *something*—even a tense, unfulfilled something—rather than *nothing*, sheer openness, love without borders, deep being without end.

Infinite love is who we really are and who we refuse to be. *This refusal is our most essential tension.* Our bittersweet sex life is a clear reflection of this push-me-pull-you drama between our deep desire to be open as love and our reflexive clench for safety and superficial self-esteem.

In sex, we desire to lose our superficial self completely in overwhelming bodily joy, but we also fear this loss of self. We long to merge with our lover so deeply that our vulnerable hearts are one light, but we also resist this oneness. We ache to let go of all protection and enter nakedly into unguarded love, but we are also afraid of this vulnerability.

We yearn and hesitate to give our deepest depth of being—which is God's depth—through sexual love. This openness of being is all there is and who we are, and yet we stand divided and protected. We refuse to trust.

Our refusal to trust is often grounded in the past: We were abused as a child. We were jilted by an ex-lover. Our partner has been selfish, distracted, closed down, or insensitive.

It is very important to address these realities in our lives through intervention, communication, therapy, supportive friends, wise teachers, and our own personal inquiry and exploration. In addition, it is often necessary to protect ourselves—physically and emotionally—from abusive and destructive relationships.

Even so, we eventually learn that emotional closure is our own action. We can be responsible for it. In any moment, we can choose to open or to close. *Nothing outside of us has the power to limit our capacity to give and receive love.* Even while pointing out perpetrators and working to heal the wounds we have suffered in the past, if our heart is not open, we are simply refusing to trust the deepest depth of our being. We are refusing to express our open and infinite nature. We are refusing to live as love in this present moment.

Love's light wants to express itself through our bodies. But even though our deepest self wants to open and live as love, our superficial self is afraid. So we hold back the spontaneous and powerful expression of love flowing through our bodies. We do this primarily by suppressing our breath.

Breath is the way our bodies make love with God. When we are willing to be love, then we are willing to breathe love. When we are unwilling to be love, when we resist the spontaneous expression of our deep and natural openness of being, then we suppress our breath. Our belly constricts. Our heart tightens. Inside, we tie ourselves in knots and become endarkened. Our entire body clenches the flow of energy that wants to shine through us. We suffer our refusal of divine openness. We suffer our refusal to live as love.

The fantasy of instant perfect sex may sell, but in reality it takes practice to undo the kinks we have spent years crimping into our bodies and emotions. Enlightened sex is a way to unbind the knots we have tightened around our heart so we can live free as love. Opening our breath is a key to untying our internal knots so that our love can fully express itself.

We can begin to open by learning to feel love's light as sexual *energy*. What does your internal sexual energy feel like?

Imagine that you come home after a day of working, tired. You lie down on the sofa and relax. You feel like you could lie there forever. Your lover walks over and sits next to you, gently rubbing your shoulders. After kneading your muscles, your lover trails his or her fingertips lightly up and down your neck, leaning over and kissing you. Your lover continues massaging you, kissing your neck, your ears, your lips.

Your breathing deepens. You begin to feel some energy moving within your body. Your lover runs his or her hands down your thighs to your feet. After massaging your feet for a while, your lover takes your toes into his or her mouth, one at a time, and sucks them gently.

You look into your lover's eyes and feel them filled with love and openness. You feel like you are being drawn into a garden of love. A few moments before, your body was exhausted and empty, a worn husk. Now, your body is filled with delight, moving with energy, breathing deeply, percolating with happiness, writhing and alive.

Your lover kisses his or her way up your feet, up your legs, up your belly to your chest. Unbuttoning your shirt, your lover kisses your nipples, and then you press your bodies together. Your lover's tongue licks your neck.

Strong energy moves through you now. Your breath is full and deep. You feel wide awake. Your pelvises are rocking together, your spines undulating, your flesh pulsating.

How can you continue to enlarge the flow of sexual energy, enjoying many whole-body orgasms, rejuvenating yourselves, opening your hearts, and surrendering as one in blissful loving? The first step involves understanding how your breath and sexual energy intertwine.

1 USE YOUR BREATH TO AROUSE AND RELAX YOUR GENITALS

Although there are many subtle aspects to your breath, two major sexual functions are the reception and release of energy. When you *inhale*, you are opening yourself and *receiving* breath and energy into your body. When you *exhale*, you are letting go and *releasing* energy. When you are born, one of your first acts is to inhale, drawing breath into the body. When you die, one of your last acts is to exhale, releasing all hold on this life. The birth and death of your genital arousal is a similar process.

Your inhalation feeds energy down into your genitals. Men who have difficulty getting or maintaining an erection and women who have dry or painful vaginas are often weak inhalers. They have difficulty receiving energy and emotion. Their belly is not open and alive, able to expand with breath energy as the full inhalation brings force down the front of their body to the genitals. These people also tend to be weaker in the world than their actual potential. Either they are unable to muster the energy to get things done, or they tend to be heady and pointed while doing them, rather than full and relaxed.

If you have trouble getting or maintaining an erection, or if your vagina tends to be dry and painful during sex, then you might benefit from strengthening your inhalation. Make sure that throughout the day, and especially during sex, your inhalations are full and deep. Draw the inhalation down the front of your body, expanding your belly with breath and filling your genitals with the inhaled energy. Your inhalation should be so full that you actually feel a pressure pushing into your genital region as the inhalation reaches its brink. With each inhalation, feel as if you are priming the pump, filling the genitals and lower abdomen with energy.

Your exhalation releases energy. Men and women who are hyper-energetic and tend toward frequent but superficial orgasms tend to be weak exhalers. They have difficulty letting go and allowing the energy to circulate throughout their entire body and beyond. They are all too ready to be filled with energy, and then, because they are unable to easefully exhale the energy or circulate it, they become anxious about releasing it through other means. They tend to be easily angered, addicted to eating frenzies and orgasm-centered sex, and often look for other ways to blow off steam. Exhalation is a form of surrender. Emotionally, weak exhalers tend to be unsurrendered in the sexual occasion and thus unable to give and receive love with profound depth of feeling.

If you have trouble postponing ejaculation or participating in sex with deep emotional surrender, then you will want to practice strengthening your exhalation. Allow your exhalations to be long, slow, and full, really letting go of all of your breath, as if you were "dying" into bliss. As you exhale, release all hold on yourself so you feel you are giving yourself totally to the moment, to your partner, and to love. Surrender yourself more deeply with each full exhalation as you offer your gifts of energy and love to your partner. Release the breath from your whole body, including the lower part, so your belly and genitals feel fully released and given in love.

To summarize, weak inhalation means weak genital arousal. Weak exhalation means weak ability to circulate energy. If you want to increase genital arousal, emphasize inhalation. If you want to decrease genital arousal, emphasize exhalation. As you inhale, open yourself to fully receive love, life, and energy. As you exhale, surrender yourself, giving yourself totally, so that no love is left ungiven. The sexual occasion provides an opportunity to practice these two primary emotional aspects of breath—reception and surrender—in an intensified fashion. Sex can fill you with so much love-energy that the pleasure and brightness becomes almost unbearable. Sex can also allow you such deep surrender that you let go of everything and give your gifts fully, offering every ounce of your love and energy.

As you practice filling and surrendering yourself through your breath during sex, you strengthen your capacity to do the same throughout the day. Your inhalations and exhalations become constant reminders to fill your body with love and energy and also to yield it all, giving your deepest gifts, holding nothing back—only to be filled again.

2 RETRAIN YOUR NERVOUS SYSTEM

To enlighten your sex, you and your partner can practice to effortlessly open as deep being while simultaneously circulating unobstructed energy. Passionate sexual desire is felt through as a transparent shimmering in the openness of being. Seeking resolves itself in an abundance of bright love.

A part of this practice is to retrain the nervous system using your breath. Most people have become accustomed to kisses and hugs, a few yanks or caresses, perhaps some licks and sucks, several minutes of warm and wet genital friction, and finally a burst of energy that releases into a peaceful, tension-free sense of relaxed depletion. This kind of sex is considered normal, even good. It is unfortunate that our culture leaves most people completely uneducated in the higher enjoyments and deeper blisses of sexuality.

In order to move to a new level of sexuality, you can retrain your nervous system. You can learn to relax your old tendencies of habitually building up and then releasing sexual tension. You can learn to use your breath to circulate unimpeded energy throughout your body and through every shade of your emotional spectrum all day. You can practice relaxing into the bliss of your deep being and then expressing it as love's light through the openness of your body. This entire process can be broken down into six steps:

1. Clear your nervous system of kinks.

Imagine energy flowing through the internal circuitry of your body like water flowing through a hose. If the hose becomes kinked, the water flow is held back and only a trickle makes it through the obstruction. Meanwhile, water pressure builds up at the site of the kink, perhaps even springing leaks and squirting out senselessly.

As an example, suppose your father was loud and cruelly abusive to you as a child. First, you were frightened, and your vulnerable heart was deeply hurt. Second, you closed your heart, held your breath, and tensed your body to protect yourself from being hurt even more. Third, your body's energy ceased to flow freely in response to masculine energy. So your internal circuitry becomes blocked by an accumulation of fear, tension, and frustrated energy: you develop an emotional kink in response to loud masculine energy.

Now, as an adult, whenever you experience the sharp, demanding aspect of masculine energy—for instance, your lover raises his or her voice and tells you what to do—your energy gets blocked. Your kink stops it from flowing. Your heart closes, your breath tightens, and your body becomes tense.

Meanwhile, pressure builds up behind the obstruction. You may feel angry, confined, hateful. Your internal "hose" of energy is about to burst. If you are in a more masculine moment, you may strike out at someone or punch a hole in the wall. If you are in a more feminine moment, you are more likely to turn your anger inward and "strike in," abusing yourself through overeating, overspending, or neglecting your responsibilities.

In addition to emotional kinks, you might have physical kinks. Perhaps through faulty exercise or inadequate breathing, you've developed rigidity in your belly. Your abdomen is no longer relaxed and open. Energy cannot flow through it. An obstruction like this can have a number of results: a lack of sexual desire;

an inability to achieve penile erection, vaginal lubrication, or orgasm; even a lack of assertiveness in social situations. Your rigid belly prevents the full force of energy from descending down the front of your body and giving you the power to act that you would otherwise have.

Besides emotional and physical kinks, mental kinks may also block your flow of energy. Perhaps you are obsessed, day after day, with certain sexual fantasies: being tied up and forced to have an orgasm, seducing your best friend's spouse, finding a lover who will never leave you. Or maybe you are stuck mulling over what someone said about you at work earlier in the day.

These mental kinks may obstruct your flow of internal energy, especially as your energy flow increases during sex. While you are trying to enjoy sex, your magnified sexual energy may get caught in dead-end loops of thoughts, hopes, and imagery, unable to complete the circuit of fullness throughout your entire body. Parts of your body may feel numb, tense, or painful. Sexually, your power will be absent and your pleasure will be thin. Your presence and love-energy will stay locked in your head, obstructed by the mental kink.

So, the first step is to unkink your emotional, physical, and mental obstructions. This can be done through many means. Because each person is unique, you must discover which methods work best for you. Usually a combination of techniques is most effective, and your daily practices may change over time as you grow and new stresses come and go from your life.

For instance, you might visit a psychotherapist to resolve some mother-issues that you can't seem to resolve on your own. In conjunction with this, you may use massage, hatha yoga, or tai chi to help open the channels of your body so your energy circulates more freely. Changing your diet may be important. Volunteer work and serving others is often a significant way to encourage a full flow of love through your body. Dancing and singing may be integral for keeping your inner channels of energy open.

Through trial and error and the guidance of those you trust, discover which treatments and therapies most precisely address your current issues and help open the kinks that are limiting you now, emotionally, physically, or mentally. Choose the practices that meet your particular needs and help you to express your deepest gifts. It is an axiom of spiritual growth that your deepest gifts are often capped by your most stubborn obstructions.

In addition to whatever other methods you choose to use, the sexual practices presented in this book may be an extremely effective means to open yourself so that you may know and express your deepest being. In the way of the superior lover, sexual energy is circulated through your body to clear out the kinks so your love can flow more freely.

2. Train your nervous system to circulate energy.

Instead of pumping the genitals till they burst, learn to circulate energy throughout the natural circuitry of the whole body. It is as if you become one huge genital, rushing with orgasmic light and energy from toe to head. Your heart opens wider and wider so that the size of your loving expands to infinity, engulfing you and your partner in an open bliss of being that renders fear and desire obsolete.

This practice involves learning to move energy through your natural internal circuitry, up the spine and down the front of the body in a continuous circular flow. You learn to use intentional muscular locks at specific places throughout your body to serve this circulation. Complete step-by-step instructions for how to circulate your internal energy are presented in Part Four.

BASIC ENERGY CIRCULATION

As energy builds in your genitals during sex, *exhale* and contract the floor of your pelvis, pulling upward slightly, as if you were trying to stop yourself from urinating. Feel or imagine your sexual energy moving *up* along the line of your spine into your head as you exhale. Then, as you *inhale,* draw the energy *down* the front of your body, so that your belly expands as it fills with energy and breath. Draw the energy all the way down to your genitals and pelvic floor.

(As described in Part Four, at times it is better to *inhale* energy up your spine and *exhale* it down your front. In any case, your energy always circulates *up your spine* and *down your front.*)

Continue breathing energy in a circle this way, contracting and pulling upward at the pelvic floor while exhaling energy up your spine and then inhaling it down the front of your body to your belly and genitals.

This circle of energy, up your spine and down the front of your body, is the way energy moves in a naturally open body. By practicing this way of breathing and moving energy, both throughout the sexual play and randomly throughout the day, you will remove obstructions to the free flow of your energy, sexually and at other times. Please see Part Four for complete instructions as well as more advanced techniques for circulating your internal energy.

With practice, your orgasms will explode upward through your body, filling you with intense bliss and light, melting all resistance so that love flows without limitation. Your tensions become liquefied and evaporated in this intensity of love and openness. Man or woman, gay or straight, your body learns to sustain long periods of orgasmic bliss that you would not have been able to handle before.

Over time, you can learn to open as love and feel through the bliss even as its intensity exceeds anything you have experienced before. Ravished by pleasure, dissolved as openness, and brightened as the force of love, your usual obstructions are loosened in an effortless profundity of being, like clouds dissolving in the clear light of the sky. Spacious peace and unbounded love may shine through you, at least for a moment, so that your sexual embrace becomes a spiritual revelation.

With regular practice, your daily life becomes transformed. Your body becomes healthier and more vital. Your mind becomes more keen, responsive, and deep. Your emotions flow alive and fluid without becoming heavy or stuck. By learning how to open yourself through the inevitable pains and pleasures of sexual play with your partner, you strengthen your capacity to stay open during the pleasures and difficulties of daily life. You learn to live at a new level of awareness, strength, and spiritual openness.

3. Train your nervous system to sustain high levels of energy.
For many people, being relaxed means being low energy. They feel at ease only when they are depleted of energy, such as after a full meal or an orgasm. They can't handle long periods of high energy without feeling hyper, stressed, or anxious. They can't wait to have a beer, chat with a friend, watch TV, stuff their faces, or masturbate.

Enlightening your sex involves cultivating the capacity to sustain high energy over long periods of time while remaining relaxed and open. It is as if the hoses through which the water flows grow wider. More water can flow through with less pressure. You can maintain ease even when great force is coursing through your body, mind, and emotions. Your body is pregnant with flexible force, like a fiercely tumescent fire hose. Your mind is still—yet agile, bright, and ready with insight. Your heart is alive, vulnerable, and responsive. You may cry one moment and laugh the next, but whatever you do, your flow of life force is strong and unimpeded.

You can look at two people, a conventional lover and a superior lover, and see the difference. Throughout the day, at work as well as in bed, the conventional lover swings between an agitated mode of frantic activity and a collapsed mode of tired depletion. The superior lover, however, steadily acts with great force and creativity—resting when appropriate but not collapsing due to an exhaustive spurt of energy.

To develop this capacity for sustained high energy, practice plugging your energy leaks and circulating the energy as it builds in your body. Don't fidget. Don't eat unnecessary snacks. Don't ejaculate or orgasm too often. Don't talk excessively. Don't watch TV or read newspapers, catalogs, books, and magazines simply due to habit. Don't grind your jaw or tap your pencil unconsciously.

If you stop depleting your energies through these habitual means, you may first notice yourself getting anxious to some degree. This is because your body is being filled with more energy than it is used to handling. In the past, you might telephone a friend or masturbate in the shower to release energy and decrease your internal force. Now, since you have plugged many of these leaks, your internal pressure builds.

You can accommodate this growing internal force by helping it flow throughout the natural circuitry of your body. Over time, you can cultivate a capacity to conduct a much larger flow of energy. Your internal "hoses" can unkink and widen, so your old trickle of energy becomes a full flow of force. You develop a much stronger ability to circulate great energy without dispersing it in TV, orgasms, chatting, snacking, and fidgeting.

4. Circulate your energy to heal and rejuvenate the body and emotions.
Once the internal energy circuits are cleared of major kinks and the energy flows through you in full force, then you can direct your heightened sexual energy for specific healings. Through visualization and intent, you can send energy to your kidneys, liver, lungs, stomach, and other internal organs. You can bring energy to parts of your body that may have been wounded by past traumas or injuries. You can open up areas of your body that have become tense or weakened by the demands of your daily lifestyle. As you read the following exercise, imagine yourself performing it.

MAGNIFYING AND CIRCULATING
YOUR HEALING ENERGY

A simple way to practice magnifying and circulating your internal energy is to stand straight with your feet parallel and about shoulder width apart, toes pointing forward. Bend your knees slightly. Hold your arms out in front of you at about heart height in a rounded position, with your elbows slightly bent and your palms facing your chest, as if you were embracing a large beach ball. Allow the tip of your tongue to rest gently against the roof of your mouth. Relax your body as much as possible while still maintaining the integrity of the posture, your feet flat, your spine elongated, your half-closed eyes gazing at the horizon.

Practice breathing in the circle just as you would practice this during sex. Inhale energy down the front of your body, filling your belly with enough force and breath to feel an internal pressure pushing against your genitals. Then contract upward with your genitals and entire pelvic floor while exhaling the energy up your spine.

To keep from becoming too rigid, smile. Smile with your face, and also feel the insides of your whole body smiling, especially your belly and chest. Continue standing with bent knees, extending your arms as if they were embracing a large ball of energy in front of your chest. Keep your lower back relaxed. You can imagine that a string from the heavens is attached to the very top of your head, pulling it up, and a thousand-pound weight is attached to the tip of your coccyx, or tailbone, pulling it down, elongating and relaxing your spine. You can relax the smile on your face but maintain the sense of your body smiling inside, especially when the posture begins to feel difficult to hold.

Holding this posture and breathing in this circle will increase your internal energy as sexual stimulation does. Some people are very sensitive to their internal energy flow and others aren't, so don't worry if you don't feel energy moving up your spine and down the front of your body at first. With practice, as your obstructions clear and your energy flows more fully, it will be easier to feel.

If you experience sharp pain in your joints, such as your knees, hips, or shoulders, then immediately come out of the posture and rest. However, trembling and rushes of heat or cold in your muscles are normal while learning to circulate your energy. If your legs begin to shake, or if your entire body shakes, that is fine and good. Stay with the exercise, holding the posture, resting your tongue against the roof of your closed mouth, always breathing through the nose, breathing your energy up your spine and down your front, smiling with the insides of your body. Practice this exercise for a few minutes a day, gradually building up until you can hold the posture for about ten minutes.

Remember to keep your heart area soft, open, and relaxed. It sometimes helps to imagine you are embracing your lover body-to-body while doing this exercise.

Once you develop some proficiency at feeling the force of your internal energy flowing up your spine and down your front, you can visualize or imagine it flowing to the parts of your body that most need it. Suppose you feel a knot in your gut from the stress of a tough day. As you inhale energy down your front, also inhale energy directly into the tension in your belly. Feel as if you are filling a balloon, expanding the knot with the force of your breath so it opens and loosens. Then, as you exhale, release the tension from the knot so it circulates freely throughout your internal circuitry. Inhale fresh energy into the knot, then exhale tension and circulate the energy. Repeat this for several minutes. If the tension from the knot feels like it wants to be released out of your body, exhale it out of your hands and feet.

In addition to bringing energy to various parts of your body, you can use this kind of standing posture to direct your heightened energy into emotional areas that require healing. If you were sexually abused as a child, for instance, you can carefully and lovingly re-create the situation of abuse with a trusted and trustable partner. Then, in the midst of the re-created traumatic situation, you can run magnified internal energy through the blocks and kinks, reopening the natural circuitry of your body.

You can do this practice in conjunction with sexual stimulation, following the instructions in Part Four, or you can move your internal energy and reopen your natural circuitry by modifying the standing exercise described above, using a sitting or lying position in order to help replicate the situation of abuse. It is best to practice these kinds of exercises under the supervision of a qualified psychological or medical professional.

By learning to circulate magnified energy through your internal circuitry with compassion and love, you can carefully dredge through the emotional and physical obstructions formed by a wide range of past wounds and recurrent memories. Physical and emotional healing can take place exceptionally quickly and thoroughly, once your body has been opened through persistent practice and you know how to circulate your energy,

With practice, you can heal deeper and deeper levels of tension-residue accumulated in your body and mind from past hurt and trauma. Meanwhile, you learn to clear daily obstructions as soon as they occur. Eventually, when you have healed enough of your *accumulated* kinks and resistances, your practice deals more or less entirely with your degree of openness or closure in the *present moment*. Being love or being unlove? That is the only question.

5. Be free consciousness, or love, in the midst of sexual energy.
It is all too easy to get lost in the energy process of sex. Sex is
sometimes so pleasurable that you can forget all else—or so dis-
gusting that you want to run. Sexual energy can be so joyfully
intense or painfully stuck that you become distracted by the
sensations or emotions. Sometimes sexual practice can seem so
interesting or so boring that you become completely engrossed
in perfecting or hating a sexual technique that you are using to try
to fix yourself or your partner.

But the primary purpose of enlightened sex is not to fix anything or anyone. Nor is it to become absorbed in sensual pleasure,
fleeting thoughts, or heavy emotions. The primary purpose of
enlightened sex is to live as love by recognizing and relaxing into
the open, unlimited, aware depth of being that you are, whether
you feel good or bad in the present moment.

When you feel through all sensation, you feel into the open
source of sensation. When you feel through all thoughts, you feel
into the open space in which thoughts occur. *When you feel through
your sexual desire or aversion, you feel into the love that is living as you.*

This open, spacious, loving nature is your true nature. The
way of the superior lover is about practicing being who you truly
are. It is not about changing yourself. It is about recognizing who
you are, deeply and really—who you already are, who you have
always been, and who you will always be. It is about becoming
stable in this recognition, so that all of your actions—throughout
the day and even during your dreams at night—radiate spontaneously from this relaxed and natural openness of being, rather
than from your stressful needs and fears.

A great aid in stabilizing this recognition is opening the energy channels of your body, which can be done very effectively

through the sexual practices we are describing. This healing process is not absolutely necessary, but most people do need to heal some internal obstructions in order to persist with adequate energy and attention in their practice of recognition.

In other words, if you are frequently distracted by the pleasures or pains of sex, then you won't have the energy or attention to persist in recognizing who you are. Sexual wounds and desires are among the greatest sources of distraction, not just during sexual embrace but throughout the day. Much of our emotional suffering is rooted in our sexual hopes and fears.

If you don't clear these knots, they can absorb your energy and nag at your attention, day and night. Rather than practicing meditation, you will fantasize about Mr. Right or your coworker's shapely ass. Rather than practicing love, you will cram your mouth with food and slather your taste buds with drink because your partner left you for another lover. Even the most advanced spiritual practitioners are often plagued by their unfinished sexual business and emotional kinks.

Therefore, the first step for most people is to clarify their sexual desires and unkink the flow of energy trapped in their emotional wounds. But once that is done, and even while it is being done, the main point of practice is to free consciousness and live as love. The breathing exercises presented here and in Part Four can be very healing and enlivening. They bring energy and natural openness to the body and emotions. But you can also get lost in these exercises, imagining that they are ultimately liberating. They are not.

Even while practicing a breathing technique, you must feel the love that is moving the whole process. Feel love's openness of light, rippling as your sensations, thoughts, and emotions. Feel the love moving you to practice enlightened sex. This same love is moving your partner, if you have one. Feel into your heart, your partner's heart, and feel every thought and sensation so fully that you suddenly find yourself opening as feeling itself.

Don't become lost in an exercise, so focused on the energy technique that you have nothing left over for the primary practice of being love, opening wide as conscious feeling. If you can't smile in the midst of your practice, you are taking it too seriously. If you can't feel the ultimate futility of energy practice — after all, your body is going to die and rot in any case — then it is easy to become addicted to the process of perfecting your energies.

You can't perfect your body, your sex, or your energy. They are all going to have their good days and bad days, until finally they dissolve in death. But you can perfect your trust of love. You can stabilize your practice of feeling through the events and sensations of every moment, so that nothing distracts you from who you really are. You simply remain as you are and always have been, conscious as your eternal and spacious nature, open as love, aware as the radiant being that you are.

You can forget the truth of your unbounded being — and forget that you have forgotten — or you can remember and practice recognizing this moment's essential openness. If you forget it and close down, then your attention begins wandering to relieve the stress of contracting your feeling. The pain of your own ongoing tension makes you look for a cure. You may begin to believe that something is missing from your life. You want to earn more money, find a better lover, or make your current partner love you more. Every moment becomes a moment of stressful need, and your attention is never free enough to feel through the doings of the moment and simply open as love's always present offering. Rather, life becomes one stress after another, and then it is time for bed. Days and nights suddenly become years. Nothing makes any real difference but the momentum is too strong to stop. Life slips by.

However, in any moment you feel through the doings, you are already aware of the open bliss of being which all your doings have been seeking. You still act, but you are no longer acting in order to become or to get. Instead, your doing radiates naturally from the core of your authentic being. Your doing *expresses* rather than *seeks* openness and love. Your sexing, for example, is a gift of love's light, rather than a needy hope to be fulfilled. You and your partner engage in sex to practice magnifying love's brightness, to celebrate love with your whole body and full range of emotions, to practice being the unbounded consciousness you are, truly and deeply.

6. Love prevails.

As your practice matures, during sex and throughout the day, love is expressed more and more fully and simply. Knots no longer bind you. Obstructions are felt through or dissolved. Energy flows without effort. You are free to devote your attention to the process of recognizing the openness of your being. You are willing to feel everything without recoiling into closure. You are free to give more love than you have ever given, because you no longer need sex or your partner's attention to fulfill you.

At this stage of practice, you no longer close down so easily. Even when your partner hurts you, whether purposefully or accidentally, you remain open. Your heart is continuously exposed. When you are hurt, you cry. When you are pleasurized, you moan. All the while, your heart remains open, vulnerable, alive, expressive, tender, fearless, unguarded. This profound heart-openness affects your lover and everyone around you. It affects your children, your friends, the space in the room, and, ultimately, the whole world.

You can still be hurt. You can still become sick. You still have good days and bad days. But it all occurs with an open heart. You don't add fear or stress to the world's fear and stress. Rather, the stressful momentum of the world is absorbed in your heart. You willingly suffer the unlove of others, because to close yourself to them is no longer an option. You know the truth of love, and you live love in spite of how much you might hurt. You are simply openness itself, creatively expressing itself through every human means, including sex.

3 USE YOUR TONGUE LIKE A CIRCUIT BREAKER

Your mouth and especially your tongue are very important parts of the natural circuit of sexual energy that flows from your genitals, up your spine, through your head, and back down the front of your body to your pelvic floor. As you practice moving sexual energy in this circular flow, you will notice the significant effects of tongue placement.

If you keep the tip of your tongue gently pressed against the roof of your mouth, your internal energy can flow through its complete circuit. Your tongue should remain in contact with the roof of your mouth through most of the sexual occasion and through most of the day. Then, your internal energy can flow from your head back down through the front of your body and through the entire circuit.

If your mouth remains open or your tongue remains apart from the roof of your mouth, your internal circuit of energy is broken. Your energy gets stopped in your head and cannot flow down your front, so you cannot relax in the fullness of your personal power and easeful sexual vitality. Unable to continue flowing, the stopped-up energy will tend to fill your head with thoughts, fears, tensions, and fantasies.

When your sexual energy cannot circulate fully, it will build up at different places in your body. Although your spine and various organs may suffer due to blocked and stagnant energy, most of the energy usually gets stuck in your head and/or genitals. If this happens, you will feel a chronic need to discharge tension through conventional genital orgasm and/or constant thinking.

Without proper tongue placement and circulation of energy, you can become chained to an addictive build-up-and-release cycle of excessive thinking and orgasm. Because your natural internal circuitry is disrupted, your energy is unable to flow freely through your whole body. You become unable to relax your thoughts and sexual urges. They build up. You become obsessed by head and tail. Therefore, be very conscious of your tongue placement.

While making love, consciously place your tongue in different positions in your mouth. Feel how you change your overall energy flow by changing the location of your tongue. Try placing the tip of your tongue at different places on the roof of your mouth: just behind your front teeth, on the middle of your upper palate, or far back on the soft part of your upper palate. What happens to the flow of energy from your genitals up your spine and into your head when you press your tongue with great force against the roof of your mouth? What happens when you just gently touch your tongue to the roof of your mouth?

Throughout most of the day, maintain contact between the tip of your tongue and the roof of your mouth in the location and with the pressure that feels best. Break this circuit only when you need to talk, laugh, eat, or consciously open your mouth for some other purpose. Notice how you feel once you get used to conscious tongue placement.

During sex, you can place your tongue directly on your lover's body to give and receive energy. You can exchange energy with your lover by placing your tongue in contact with your lover's tongue, lips, genitals, nipples, neck, ear, feet, belly button—any part of the body at all.

Start by placing the tip of your tongue gently on the side of your lover's neck. Now, very slowly, move your tongue, dragging its tip across your lover's skin, noticing how it affects the energy in his or her body. After using your tongue gently in this way, begin to press your tongue more forcefully into your lover's neck, as if you were trying to reach into your lover's heart with your tongue.

Gauge the depth, pressure, and style of tongue stroke by your lover's moment-to-moment response. Don't just listen to your lover's moans and look at how his or her body is moving, but actually learn to feel the flow of your lover's internal energy. Although it might seem nebulous at first, with practice you will be able to feel, in great detail, the energy flows within your lover's body as you open your own body and learn to merge your heart and breath with your lover's.

Continue by exploring your lover's mouth with your tongue. What happens when you press on the roof of your lover's mouth with your tongue? Try tongue-to-tongue contact. Play with pressing your lover's upper lip between your tongue and lips. Feel yourself exchanging cool feminine and hot masculine energy with your partner through your tongue.

The tongue and genitals share many similarities. They are both superlative givers and receivers of energy. They are both critical links in the circuit of energy through your own body, as well as in the circuit of energy through your partner's body. Used skillfully, they can magnify the force of sexual energy in both you and your partner. Used unskillfully, they can unwittingly misdirect energy, leaving you feeling depleted from lost energy or tense from blocked energy.

In general, during sex your tongue should be either pressed lightly against the roof of your own mouth to complete your inner energy circuit or used consciously to move energy through your lover's body. The secret is to feel the effect, moment by moment, that your tongue is creating, both for yourself and for your lover. In this way, your tongue moves skillfully to create artful loving, rather than flopping about like the clumsy want of an eager dog.

4 USE YOUR EYES TO DIRECT ENERGY

Your eyes are strong regulators of energy. What you do with your eyes strongly influences where your energy goes.

For instance, if you are trying too hard to "love" during sexual practices, then this excessive effort might show in your bulging, wide-open eyes, staring into your partner's eyes. During such a love stare, your energy will accumulate behind your eyes and in your head, rather than circulate freely throughout your body. Your head will look like it is about to pop. A truly loving gaze is more often a relaxed gaze, not the "love stare" so common amongst good-hearted "spiritual" people trying to be loving.

If your stare is stuck on one part of your partner's body, then your energy will also become stuck. There is nothing wrong with looking at your partner's sexual organs. In fact, beholding each other's sexual form is an important part of making love. But if you become fixated, obsessively staring at one part of your partner's body for too long, then your energy will become fixated. Rather, drink deeply of your partner's beauty, allowing your gaze to travel all over his or her body, freely, relaxedly, with great appreciation but no rigid fixation.

Relaxed eyes help your energy to be relaxed. If your eyes are moving erratically all over, your thoughts will also move erratically all over. Your eye movements should be like silk across your lover's skin: smooth, loving, and gentle. If your eye movements become jerky and stressed, so will your thoughts, feelings, and breath.

Notice if you are holding tension in the muscles around your eyeballs or temples during sex. Stay alert, but relax the eyes in a loving gaze, not a stressful stare. As sexual stimulation becomes intense, you may find yourself squinting or otherwise adding tension to your eyes. Practice keeping your eyes relaxed, even during the height of sexual stimulation. In this way, your energy is able to flow more freely throughout your entire internal circuitry without getting stuck in the tension of your head and face.

When you close your eyes, your energy will tend to go inward. Sometimes this is appropriate. Often, however, people close their eyes to get away from the relational demand of sexuality, as if they were masturbating by themselves. Closing your eyes may move you toward fantasy rather than the actuality of you and your lover. Closed eyes may also orient you toward your own bodily sensations, limiting your capacity to feel into and through your lover.

Take care to use your eyes consciously. Just as you should keep the tongue relaxedly pressed against the roof of your mouth unless you are consciously choosing to do otherwise, your eyes should remain open and relaxed unless you are consciously choosing to use your eyes in some other specific fashion.

A primary way to use your eyes while making love is to gaze deeply into your partner's eyes. Feel the love within your partner through his or her eyes. Even if your partner seems emotionally closed, do your best to feel the openness and love behind your partner's fear or tension. By seeing through your partner's layers of resistance, you can consciously connect to the love deep in your partner's heart and bring it more and more to the fore.

As your loving penetrates your partner's depth, and his or her resistances melt, your love meets your partner's. Your openness merges with his or her openness. Together, your loving becomes one. In moments like this, love is beholding love through the eyes of you and your partner. *There is no difference, just one love, expressed through two bodies.* This is enlightened sex.

If you are ever moved to close your eyes temporarily during sex, you can still use your closed eyes correctly. Don't focus your vision as if you were looking at the backs of your eyelids. Instead, while your eyes are closed, focus your gaze at infinity. That is, while closed, your eyes should be looking far away, as if gazing deeply into a black night sky. A deep gaze will open your attention through the sensations of the moment, relax the tension of your mind, and foster a deep and free flow of energy through your body.

Just as you use your eyes throughout the sexual occasion, use your eyes consciously during orgasm as well. As you come to orgasm, or as your partner does, keep your eyes relaxed and open. Continue gazing deeply into each other's eyes. Instead of closing your eyes, see and be seen in the midst of orgasm. Show your ecstasy and see your partner's.

In the very throes of orgasm, give and receive love with your partner completely, through your whole body and through your open eyes gazing deeply into your partner's. There is nothing to hide and no need to have a "private" orgasm behind closed eyes. Occasionally, you may want to close your eyes during orgasm, especially if you are just learning to feel the energies flowing in your body. But as a general rule, keep your eyes open, deeply but easefully gazing into your partner's eyes.

Occasionally, during sex, allow your eyes to turn upward, as if you were looking at the center of your forehead. Your eyelids can be open or shut while your eyeballs are looking up. This upward gaze helps your energy move from your genitals up your spine, thus increasing the possibility of upward orgasms of long and deep bliss rather than downward ones of quick release.

As you look up with your eyes while contracting your pelvic floor and exhaling your energy upward along your spine, it is also quite possible that you will feel yourself "leaving your body" out through the top of your head. After this upward ecstasy, always complete the circle by inhaling the energy forcefully back down the front of your body, reengaging full-bodied love play with your partner.

Part Two:
Orgasm

I first learned how to circulate my internal energy in a shopping mall when I was a young teenager. After this learning occurred, my relationships to sexuality, to women, and specifically to orgasm changed drastically.

I was about twelve years old, an uncoordinated, toothpick-thin bookworm. One day my parents dropped my best friend and me off at the local mall, where we spent many of our after-school hours in the bookstore, devouring everything we could find on psychic phenomena, esoteric religions, and spiritual practices from other cultures.

On this particular bookstore visit, I began looking through some paperbacks about Tibetan lamas living in the Himalayas who had exceptional control over their bodies and minds. These Tibetan holy men would sit motionless in the snowy mountains with a wet sheet—which quickly froze—wrapped around their otherwise naked bodies. Then they would proceed to melt the frozen sheet by generating heat through the flow of their internal energy. They would spend years alone in caves, silently contemplating their true nature of pristine awareness. They would practice maintaining clear consciousness all night through their sleep and dreams. They were my heroes.

As I was staring into one of these books, I felt the presence of someone standing nearby. Too nearby. I turned to see a huge fat man, mostly bald, his belly straining against a dirty T-shirt. I immediately had visions of the child molesters and kidnappers my parents had warned me about. My heart started beating hard.

"Do you like those kinds of books?" the child molester asked me.

I swallowed. "Yes," I said, too frightened to run, too embarrassed to call for help.

"I can see that you like them. Put your hand on my shoulder," he ordered me.

By now, my best friend had put down his book and come over to where I stood facing this weird man, who seemed like an overweight sixty-five-year-old bum. Definitely a pervert, I thought.

"Go ahead," he repeated, "put your hand on my shoulder."

I felt queasy. I wanted to walk away but my legs were rubbery. I just stood there, looking at this guy, sure he was about to kidnap or hurt me. I felt helpless.

He grabbed my hand and put it on his shoulder. I felt very strange and suddenly self-conscious to be in this mall, in this bookstore, standing paralyzed with my hand on this weirdo's shoulder, while all the supposedly normal people walked about in their shopping trance, not even noticing us. The whole situation felt very unreal and dreamlike.

"Now," the big-bellied old man said, more quietly, "push."

I finally spoke up. "What do you mean?"

"Try to push me backward."

I was too scared to move. I was not about to push on a total stranger whom I didn't even want to be touching.

He grabbed my arm and pulled it toward him, as if to demonstrate what I was supposed to do. Okay, I decided. I guess there is no harm in a little push. If this guy tried anything strange, I could yell out; the mall was filled with people who would come to my rescue. Or so I hoped.

I pushed.

"Harder," he said.

So I pushed harder. He didn't budge.

"Push as hard as you can," he said.

I pushed. I really pushed. As hard as I could. He didn't move an inch. He didn't move an eighth of an inch.

"Now I'm going to stand on one leg. Push as hard as you can."

Bending his knee, he lifted one leg off the ground, my hand still on his shoulder. I didn't want to push this guy over and hurt him, even if he was a pervert. So I gave just a little nudge. And then a harder nudge. Finally I pushed him with all my teenage might. His body didn't even wobble.

He smiled and looked deep into my eyes. I realized something funny was going on.

Still looking into my eyes, he took my other arm by the wrist and placed my free hand on his other shoulder. Now I had a hand on both shoulders as he continued to stand on one leg. Again, he asked me to try to push him over.

By now I was less frightened, though still wary, and damned if I wasn't going to push this guy over. I planted my feet firmly on the floor, steadied myself, leaned into him, and pushed as hard as I could. It felt like pressing against a marble wall. I finally gave up and took my hands off his shoulders. After my friend tried pushing him over with the same results, the old man put both feet back on the ground and spoke to us matter-of-factly.

"A few years ago, I had a heart attack and a stroke, and I lay paralyzed in a hospital bed. The doctors told me I would never walk again. But I was determined to recover. A friend of mine left me a book on yoga at the hospital. It was the kind of book you boys have probably seen in this very bookstore. I had the nurse open the book and show me the pictures of yoga postures inside. Even though I couldn't move, I would imagine myself doing the exercises in the book. All day, every day, instead of watching TV or worrying about my recovery, I visualized myself practicing these exercises. Lying paralyzed in that hospital bed, I didn't have much else to do.

"Eventually, after weeks of visualization, I could move an inch. Then two inches. Six months later, I was able to sit up by myself. Now, I can stand on one leg and you boys can't even push me over. It's all about knowing how to use your internal energy. You can do it too."

Right there, in the bookstore, he taught my friend and me some basic exercises to direct our internal energy. Within ten minutes, I was able to move so much energy through my arm that my friend couldn't bend it. Nor could I bend his. With a few more minutes of practice, we even gained a modicum of proficiency at the one-leg trick. It was all a matter of circulating internal energy correctly, something I had read about in books, but had never seen or felt directly. Now this strange man, whom I had taken for a pervert, had shown us how to consciously direct our internal energy. For real. And it worked.

He smiled as my friend and I practiced what he had taught us, testing our newfound skills. Then I looked up to thank him, but he was gone. Neither of us ever saw him again.

The practices this man taught us became a part of my daily life, like brushing my teeth. In the few years following the bookstore experience, I learned to play with the flow of my own internal energy, telling my friends to try to push me over, balancing for long periods on one leg, practicing various breathing exercises while sitting alone in my room, and even trying to generate heat in my body like the Tibetans I had read about.

Eventually, other aspects of adolescent life came to dominate my consciousness. Hormones started coursing through my body and my mind became preoccupied with girls. Confusion ruled the day and fantasy ruled the night.

As a pimply teenager, I found women totally confusing. I had no idea why they did what they did. There were times when I was busy doing homework and my girlfriend pounced on me, pressing her wet mouth all over me, grabbing my crotch, humping my thigh, and moaning. Naively, I assumed she wanted sex. However, when I dropped what I was doing and returned her fervor, she suddenly seemed less interested. I would be throbbing and on fire; she would coolly walk away. Angry and frustrated, I wondered why she jumped on me in the first place. I had no idea what was going on.

Occasionally, we would actually have sex.

As I lay on top of her, meekly thrusting, she would often push against my naked chest with her hands, seeming to resist me. So, naturally, I would pull back. "No, you idiot," she conveyed with the exasperated look on her face, "when I push you away, I want to feel you taking me deeper." So I would force myself into her, ravish her hard and deep, and she would love it. And then, a few seconds later, I would notice that she was not loving it anymore. What was I supposed to do? Harder? More gentle? Give her space? Overpower her? What did she want?

If I was too careful, she'd complain that I needed to be more passionate and sexually aggressive. If I was too forceful, she'd complain that I wasn't sensitive enough. When I finally figured out what she wanted, I'd do it, and she'd hate it. When I gave up all hope and just had sex with her without trying, she would suddenly plead my name and convulse in waves of orgasm. I was totally lost. Masturbation was a lot easier than this.

By myself, I could lie in bed at night and masturbate, fantasizing about a woman who gave me exactly what I wanted. I would imagine being with her, stroke myself, spurt, and go to sleep.

Eventually, my girlfriend and I broke up. One night a few weeks later, after my family went to sleep, I made a selection from my cherished stash of girlie magazines, lay on the bed, and began masturbating. But instead of fantasizing about the women in the magazine, I suddenly became excruciatingly aware of the energy flowing through my internal circuitry. This happened quite unexpectedly.

I had more or less forgotten about the old-man-in-the-mall's internal energy practices when I became preoccupied with girls. Now, it was all coming back with a vengeance. Streams of energetic force shot through me while I masturbated. With eyes closed, I saw within myself an exquisite internal circuitry through which energy flowed like a river of light.

I could see with my internal eye and feel with my body how pumping my penis increased the flow of this river of energy. Furthermore, I could see and feel how sitting all day at school, slumped with a sunken chest, had blocked the flow of energy around my heart and solar plexus. It became obvious how I could change my breath and posture to open these blocks.

After about an hour of experimenting with my internal energy flow, I was ready to stop masturbating and go to sleep. I looked at the girlie magazine and imagined myself with the perky blonde centerfold from Wisconsin. I jerked hard and fast and ejaculated.

It was as if the light in the room suddenly became dim. My internal brightness dulled, too. My breathing became more shallow and weak. Even though I was lying in bed, the slackened energy made me feel like I was slumping.

I was amazed. Orgasms had always felt good to me. Really good. They relieved me of sexual tension and left me feeling relaxed. But now I realized that this relaxation was actually depletion. I felt less stressed because I had less energy flowing through me. I got out of bed and tried to do some of the exercises the old man in the bookstore had taught us, but my energy was too low. A baby would have been able to push me over. I got back in bed and went to sleep.

For many months, I continued masturbating, but without ejaculation. I discovered inner ecstasies and nuances of energy flow that I hadn't experienced when I first learned about internal energy from the old man in the mall, before I had become sexually active.

Eventually, I found a new girlfriend. I wasn't expecting it, but the first time we hugged I felt the energy flowing through *her* body as we embraced. It was as if I had x-ray vision; I could feelingly see the circuitry within her body. I could feel where her energy was flowing full and where it was blocked. As I hugged her, I changed my position and my breathing in order to help her energy flow more fully. I felt how our emotional closure also closed our energy, and how opening in love served to open our flow of energy.

After our hug, she stepped back and I noticed her eyes were moist. We looked into each other's eyes and felt each other, vulnerable, opened, and astonished.

Something that was previously confounding was now so obvious that I couldn't believe I had never seen it before. My girlfriends had always been sensitive to the internal flow of energy, to the bodily flow of love. Energetically, it was as if they could see and I was blind.

Their shifting moods—upset, anger, lust, lack of interest—had, in effect, been a kind of test: Would I continue to be an energetically disadvantaged nerd, trying to reduce everything to words and mentalized communication, giving up when their emotional flows didn't fit into my mental boxes? Or would I feel their deep flows of energy—which spoke the heart's true desire—and dance with the push and pull of their moods so we could both relax in love? Usually, because I didn't know any better, I had given up in exasperation.

Now everything was falling into place. The old man in the bookstore had taught me that true power is not muscular but energetic: my friend could easily bend my arm when I used only my muscles to resist, but when I felt the energy flowing through my arm like an infinite rod of light, he could not move it. I realized that I had been using my mental muscles to try to figure out and change my girlfriends' moods. But their emotional flows of energy were much more powerful than my seemingly more "muscular" mind. My girlfriends bent me every time. Because I didn't know what to do, I took the easy way out and masturbated. But now things had changed.

A few evenings after our first hug, I was in my bedroom with my new girlfriend. She stood a few feet away from me, her eyes downcast. Instead of being my usual doltish self and asking her what was wrong, I very slowly moved closer to her, feeling her energy every inch of the way. For a moment, I felt her energy close down, so I stopped moving. I breathed with her rhythm, synchronizing my breath with hers, feeling her mood through and through, until my feeling reached her heart. I felt what she felt. Her deep needs—previously so mysterious to me—were now as intimate as mine. She relaxed and I continued moving toward her, ever so slowly.

Step by step, feeling through her shifting moods into her heart, breathing her breath, feeling her energy, I embraced and kissed her. No part of her escaped my feeling. I knew what it meant to love with the whole body. I could feel her deepest heart, her toes, her ears. I was able to feel her ever-changing currents of energy tingling, warming, and slithering throughout her body. Soon we were making love.

As I lay on top of her, she made a face and turned away. Instead of thinking about what I should do, I felt into her. I breathed her energies. I opened my heart more widely and extended my love into her body more deeply, feeling all of her.

She was incredibly responsive to my every twitch and nuance of intention, which demanded total presence on my part. If I became lost in my own sensations, even for a brief moment, her heart would recoil as if I had just wounded it, and I would need to gently reestablish trust, loving her, coaxing her energy to return to the fore.

If I averted my eyes or held my breath too abruptly, even for a moment, her energy flow would diminish and become choppy. What seemed to me to be tiny and insignificant—whether I touched her breasts with my fingers or palm, whether I breathed through my nose or my mouth, whether I allowed my weight to sink into her body or held myself up on my elbows—had profound and immediate effects on her energy flow and heart openness.

No wonder I previously had so much trouble knowing what my former girlfriend had wanted. What she wanted—what she needed in terms of energy — changed moment by moment. Sometimes she might need a delicate kiss on her neck to help her open. In the very next moment, she might need a ravishing thrust to deepen her surrender — or maybe such sudden passion would close her down entirely. It all depended on being able to feel her moment-to-moment flow of energy and openness of heart — which, in the past, I hadn't been able to feel at all. I didn't know how to open my whole body in love and allow myself to be one with my lover.

Now that I was no longer driving toward an ejaculation, lost in my own sensations, I was able to breathe and move with my girlfriend. Our energy combined in trustful harmony. She could feel my presence pervading every inch of her body. She could feel my loving intention, my constancy and fullness. So, she let her heart open ever wider, teaching me love beyond what I had ever allowed myself. Her surrendered body became an inviting extension of her open heart. I was awed. And humbled.

Earthquakes of orgasms rendered her senseless in the intensity of love. Her convulsions, spittle, tears, and cries, her uncontrollable bliss-contortions of body and emotion all magnified my internal energy. This only demanded more presence on my part lest I ejaculate and put a sudden end to the magnification of energy and love that, for her, seemed endless.

Her utter surrender and bodily ecstasy were far more attractive and energizing to me than any picture in a magazine could possibly be. Her loving was so total, expressing itself so freely and powerfully through her entire body, that I was called to yield my separateness over and over again into the unending openness of our loving.

Of course, the next minute, or the next day, she might surprise me with a sudden change of mood. If I had ejaculated too frequently, or if my own internal energy was low for other reasons, then the weight of her mood would bend me. I would attempt to figure out what was happening and right myself through mentally muscular means: argument, analysis, and insistence. But her energy was usually stronger than my mind; even if she agreed with me, in the end I would be worn down. Too weakened to stand unmovable in love and humor, I might walk away from her moods, seeking solitude or refuge with my less energetically weighty male buddies—who were all too ready to smile, shake their heads, and commiserate with me.

But if my internal energy was full, then my girlfriend's moods of push and pull would not sway me. I could relax my mind and stand on one leg of love, feel through her mood into her true need, combine myself with her energies, and dissolve in the openness of our love. If my energy was circulating without obstruction, I would have the stamina necessary to engage with her emotions as long as necessary, neither petering out nor resenting her, but embracing her in love.

I have had teachers in my life who have revealed more profound truths than those shown to me by the old man in the bookstore, but it is to him that I owe the capacity to combine myself with my lover in a way that magnifies rather than depletes our energy and opens us in love. It has been a long time since I first received his lessons, and I am still enjoying the ongoing process of learning. But my relationship to sexual loving has been changed irrevocably by his gifts.

Understanding your relationship to sexual energy—and especially to orgasm—is a key to cultivating your depth of energy and strengthening your capacity to open in love regardless of mood or mind. Straight or gay, how can men increase their personal stamina and spiritual sensitivity by converting ejaculative release into multiple, whole-body orgasms? How can women fulfill their body's desire for love-bliss by opening and relaxing into full-blown clitoral, vaginal, and cervical orgasms?

First, we will look at how men can enlarge their orgasmic potential and why they might want to. Then we will look at women's potential for orgasmic delight. I have included personal accounts with some of the following descriptions in order to help illustrate the sexual experiences and practices.

5 BYPASS EJACULATIONS FOR GREATER PLEASURE

I have been making love with my partner for quite a while, and I am on the verge of ejaculating. I feel like I will explode any moment. I want to release the pressure that is building inside me. I know it will feel so incredibly good. For a few seconds. And then I will feel depleted and empty, ready for sleep, drifting in the emptiness of post-orgasmic peace.

My urge to orgasm is climbing, climbing, nearing the crest of the mountain, just about ready to peak in intense pleasure, before I let go and roll down, down, down the other side. Then it will be over.

I want this orgasm. I want it bad. I want to spurt it out and fill my woman with my seed. I want to feel the release of this sexual pressure building inside me. I want the pleasure.

I have been here before. A quick wad-blowing seizure and consequent emptiness. Sleep. Get up in the morning. It's all quite routine.

"What do I really want?" I ask deeply in my heart. Even more than this impending moment of release, what do I want, through and through? What have I always wanted? What do I want from my work, from my sexing, from my friends, from my family? What do I want altogether in my life, more than anything else?

An ejaculation is not it. What I really want is a depth of openness far beyond the cycle of tension and release afforded by a genital spurt. I want to love so profoundly, relax so deeply, and abide so effortlessly in the freedom of open consciousness that I cease being afraid, unfulfilled, or separate at heart.

My whole life revolves around this need. I am constantly seeking love, fulfillment, or freedom from stress and fear. Yet everything I do to alleviate my suffering and increase my happiness seems only to prolong the shallow torture. As I grow older, I find myself settling for familiar comforts. Seeking profound fulfillment seems futile.

Nothing I do, no event, ever gives me what I really want. And yet I remain riveted to the sequence of events, planned and unplanned, that unfold as my life, as if they are leading somewhere fundamentally different from this present moment, something final that will end my search.

Ejaculation epitomizes this need. I am on the verge of coming, of real pleasure, and I can feel my attention being corralled by this possibility. I do not feel my partner lying vulnerably beneath me. I do not feel the dying, pain-wracked souls eking out an existence in less fortunate places on this earth, people whose suffering I can hardly imagine. Instead, I am pumping my genitals in my partner's warm wetness, focusing entirely on my imminent ejaculative release.

I especially do not feel the truth of my deep being, which is already—right now, just as it is—free, open, and unbound. My very nature is unlimited, undefined, unspeakably absolute. But instead of feeling free as this infinity, my attention is targeted on my impending squirt. All that came before me, and all that happens outside my bedroom, and all that is right here and now—the immense openness of this very moment, its simple suchness, the transparent effulgence that appears right now as my experience—all of this is ignored so I can focus on my ejaculation. I am a slave to genital need.

Feeling this, recognizing how I am contracting attention and creating suffering in this otherwise open and free moment, I stop clinging. The spotlight of my attention, previously narrowed on the event of my impending ejaculation, widens into a broad flood of light, shining through the entire event — my lover, the bed, the room, the world, the past, and the future. In this wideness of space, the genital urge also widens, so that my whole body is relaxed, opened out, and filled with flows of unkinked energy.

I relax my belly and chest so my breath can flow unobstructed, with full force and great ease. I relax my jaw, face, and eyes so the whole front of my body is soft, round, alive, and vibrant, not stiff or tight.

I inhale deeply down the front of my body, as if drawing energy from my head, down my face, through my throat and chest, into my belly, and down to my genitals. Then I contract the floor of my pelvis so it becomes like a trampoline. As the energy comes down my front, I bounce it off my pelvic floor with an upward intention and muscular contraction of my anus, genitals, and perineal area. Exhaling, I shoot the energy back from my genitals and upward along my spine. As the orgasm energy glides up my spine, my eyes turn up and great blisses rush in an upward direction through my body, through my head, and up, up, up, as if into a great space of light.

My breath becomes suspended in this upward realm of light. All time is made into space and even this wide realm disappears in a vastness beyond form. Our bodies hang lightly below like eaten fruit in a vanished dream.

With the returning inhale, my belly swells and sucks me back down, deep into the body. Face open, throat open, chest open, I descend into the fullness of my belly, pressed against my lover. Our hearts open so wide we are both swallowed in a surrender that loosens all edges into one open.

All seeking is resolved. I rest as the space that I am, as does my lover. Our sexual play continues, but now it echoes in a wall-less chamber of huge love. The craving that made me tense with ejaculative need dissolves spontaneously in the openness of being, who I am, who she is, rippling as this moment.

The energy that previously wanted to squirt out my penis now shoots up our spines, bathing our egglike bodies in luminous bliss, softening our hearts into the wide gentleness of love. Again and again, orgasmic energy shoots up our spines, through our brains, and then cascades down, floating into our bodies like so many heavy feathers of full surrender.

My chest and belly relax and fill even more as energy continues pouring down. I feel pregnant with energy. Full and unobstructed, like the deep blue sea. This is who I am. This is who my lover is. Always. This full nothing, this cognizant emptiness alive as all forms. Effortless and all.

My practice is to stabilize in this recognition by noticing this openness again and again, gently, whenever my attention narrows or my heart closes.

The deep peace I have always wanted is not in events. No wad of jism or cash can deliver it. No woman or absence of woman can instigate it. It *is*, exactly as I am, regardless of what comes and goes. In it, *as* it, all forms hover like waves of heat in the desert air, like sweetness in the space of taste. Ejaculation is made trivial in this endless depth of love. All sexing shimmers in the open of wide being.

•   •   •

Common genital ejaculation is probably one of the most pleasurable and addictive things a man has ever experienced—until he has experienced a whole-body orgasm, a brain orgasm, energy shooting up his spine, or total dissolution with his lover in bliss. Until he has experienced these greater pleasures, a man is unlikely to want to give up his ejaculative fix.

Bypassing the ejaculation to allow deep, multiple, whole-body orgasms requires both technical practice and spontaneous feeling-sensitivity. Technical practice alone may allow you to bypass ejaculation, but your sexing will be dry and not open. Sensitivity alone may allow you to feel through the edges of the moment into innate openness, but your bodily habits will remain unchanged and so your realization of openness will remain short-lived; you will be distracted by your familiar emotional neediness and physiological obstructions.

Technical practice involves learning to circulate energy down the front of your body and upward along your spine in coordination with the breath. Contracting your pelvic floor allows you to seal it against leakage as well as "bounce" energy upward. Turning your eyes upward sometimes helps energy to flow up along your spine into and through your head. Pressing your tongue gently against the roof of your mouth allows energy to flow more fully down from your head through your throat and heart into your belly. Softening your belly and chest allows your front to conduct and hold more energy. The details of this technical practice are presented in Part Four.

All day, whenever you can remember to do so, it is helpful to practice receiving energy fully while inhaling deep into your belly, as well as releasing energy fully while exhaling upward along the spine. You can also practice contracting your pelvic floor periodically throughout the day. Then, when you are in the midst of sex, the basic circulation of breath and energy will already be in place.

But none of this will fulfill you profoundly unless you are also practicing love. Love itself is a practice. It is something you can do over and over, improving your capacity to love more freely with fewer bounds, even through difficult moments. *Unless you deepen your capacity to love, the technical sexual practices will only make you into a non-ejaculatory robot of mechanical thrust and breath.*

Practicing love often means feeling through fear: intentionally opening yourself when you would rather close down, giving yourself when you would rather hide. Love means recognizing yourself as the open fullness of this moment regardless of its contents — trenchant thoughts, enchanting pleasures, heavy emotions, or gnawing pains — and surrendering all hold on the familiar act you call "me."

The natural momentum of your deep being is more and more to live as love. Yet it is all too easy to collapse from love and limit yourself to familiar cycles of mind, desire, emotion, and fear. It is easy to narrow the naturally compassionate wideness of this moment.

If you are like most people, most of the time, you are probably reducing love, over and over, in similar ways: Your genitals are about to burst from pleasure, so this moment of love becomes reduced to attention on a few square inches of pressure and juice. Your partner criticizes you and so love collapses into hurt, closure, and anger. You try oh-so-hard to bypass ejaculation and end up diligently narrowing love into mechanical effort, forgetting to feel your partner, the room, and the entire world.

Love is recognizing, now, that without changing anything whatsoever, the openness of this moment is who you are. Love is practiced by noticing the transparent feel-through of this moment, by relaxing as the cognizant openness that you are, not by trying to force yourself to be more loving.

Open love is your natural state, unless fear intervenes and stress follows. No amount of technical sexual practice will relieve you of this stress; only the practice of love will cut the roots of fear and undermine your addiction to de-stressing through ejaculation.

The superior lover is one who practices authentic loving in the form of his or her chosen lifestyle, rather than stopping short and building a comfortable cage of familiar habits inside the confines of fear. Enlightened sex involves technical exercises to retrain the body's energy, but primarily it is a matter of practicing love, feeling through the limits on love, and unguardedly being the vulnerable openness that is your true nature, over and over and over—during sex, with family, and at work—so the reflex of separation ceases to bind the heart to the familiar sense of stress that we call "me." Only the unguarded heart, relaxed as the whole of this moment, is willing to feel as the openness that consumes birth and death.

6 RETRAIN THE ADDICTION TO EJACULATION

Most men have become addicted to ejaculatory orgasms through at least three routes.

1. Evolution.

If a man didn't ejaculate, then he didn't make babies. You can be pretty sure that your father ejaculated. Likewise, your father's father ejaculated. And so on, all the way back. We are the result of tens of thousands of years of human thrust and spew, not to mention the furry ejaculations of our primate forefathers. Evolutionarily, all men, straight and gay, have inherited their ancestors' predisposition toward ejaculatory orgasms.

And quick ones at that. Imagine that ten thousand years ago you are a man having sex with a woman in the wilderness. Or, perhaps yesterday, you are a man in bed with your woman hoping to make her pregnant while your three children are in the other room playing with a video game. In terms of being a successful impregnator, would it be better to be able to ejaculate in a few minutes, before tigers or toddlers pounce on you and your lover? Or would it be better, in terms of making babies, if it took you an hour or so to ejaculate?

Obviously, the former. It may not be romantic, it may not be the deepest way to have sex, but in terms of reproduction, a man who ejaculates quickly—and frequently—will be most successful. Over evolutionary time, men who were fast and frequent ejaculators probably had more babies on the average, and thus propagated their genes more, than men who were slow and infrequent ejaculators.

So, today, you see the descendants of these successful re-producers: modern men who ejaculate relatively quickly and frequently, men addicted to ejaculation.

2. Early sexual experience.

You are a young teenage boy. Your friends teach you how to mas-turbate, or maybe you figure it out for yourself. You are in the bathroom, sitting on the toilet. One hand holds your mother's women's magazine, opened to a bra advertisement. Your other hand holds your young sexual organ, tumescent and about to burst.

You whack and yank for a few minutes and spew your goo, wipe yourself clean, and hurry off to dinner. At night, before falling asleep, you lie in bed and repeat the process, imagining a pretty girl from school standing before you, naked and sexy.

Thus you train your body, your nervous system, and your mind. Stroke, stroke, ooh, goo. Stroke, stroke, ooh, goo. Day af-ter day, year after year, your daily ritual sets the course for your sexual future.

Now you have grown into young adulthood. Let's say you are heterosexually oriented. You finally have your first real girl-friend. You are in bed together. You have imagined this moment a million times. You put your penis inside her, and her warm, wet vagina feels a lot better than your dry hand. You know what to do: stroke, stroke, ooh, goo.

After several years of marriage, she knows the routine, too. You can't seem to help it. It's what you do. It's sex. And you need it sometimes, badly. Once a day, three times a week, once a month, whatever is your habit: stroke, stroke, ooh, goo.

Your teenage years of masturbation have conditioned your body.

Erection and stimulation lead to ejaculation. And a pretty quick one at that. While your genitals are being stimulated, you fantasize, think, imagine girls, women, body parts, acts of naked vengeance.

This round of erection, friction, fantasy, and ejaculation continues unabated in adulthood, only now you sometimes do it inside your lover. Your sexual life is still largely a subjective affair, a hidden bathroom or bedroom indulgence, your fantasies pretty much the same as when you were a teenager. Your penis, when stimulated long enough, still feels like it needs to ejaculate. You trained your body and mind in this sequence as a teenager, and now you are addicted to it. Maybe you don't do it as often as when you were a teenager, but you are still addicted.

3. Improper life habits.

Some days, you feel like you *must* ejaculate. You've eaten too much salt or too much protein, and your body needs to release the diet-induced pressure. Your breathing is shallow and tense, and stress builds up in your body, needing to be discharged. You've been thinking about the sexy coworker in the office next to yours, and the movement of sexual thoughts has slowly accumulated into the restlessness of a minor storm, soon to be a gale of need.

Your habits of diet, breath, posture, and mind create an internal turbulence that seeks to be relieved. Your addiction to ejaculation is fueled throughout the day by these stress-creating habits. You are lying in bed, unable to sleep, a bit agitated, and you know the peace that lies on the other side of shooting your wad, relieving yourself of desire, tensions, and thought.

However, fast and frequent ejaculation is not necessary, at least not in the way it seems to most men. Ejaculation can be an option, useful if you want to have babies or as an occasional means to balance your internal energy. But beyond that, it is simply an addiction built upon evolutionary, adolescent, and daily habits of body and mind.

Sex can be a time of total dissolution in love. Sex can bathe every cell in your body with light, bliss, and life force. Sex can be an ecstatic practice of open-hearted communion and surrender to infinity. Or, sex can be ten or twenty minutes of genital stimulation ending in a spasm of biological relief.

You are no longer on the toilet, a young wanker wonking his gazonka for quick relief before dinner. You are an adult man, making love with your lover, aware that life is short and in the end nothing matters but love. Every moment is a word in your life story. You can write it quick and cheap, or you can wreak poetry from the depth of your heart.

Ejaculation is addictive. Once you start having ejaculations with some habitual frequency, it's hard to stop. You will tend to ejaculate more or less on schedule, even if you don't want to. Even if you have practiced all the proper exercises for opening your internal energy channels and circulating your sexual energy, you can still become addicted to spilling your semen through sex or masturbation. You will come right to the point of ejaculation, and instead of bypassing it in a deeper realization of sexual energy, you will think, "Well, I might as well come this time."

On the other hand, once you stop ejaculating for a while, it is much easier to bypass ejaculation by choice. If you have had non-ejaculatory sex for several weeks, it is much easier to choose not to ejaculate. Then, you can use your abundant energy to consistently deepen and strengthen your sexual power of love as well as your ability to be fully conscious, moment by moment, and true to your deepest purpose, spiritually, professionally, with friends, and with family.

For most men, becoming a superior lover involves retraining the addiction to ejaculation. When sex becomes an ecstatic and intensely pleasurable art of spiritual communion in love, then your ejaculation is naturally regulated by your breath and heart-feeling, rather than by your old habits of solitary fantasy and accumulated stress.

If you want a deep life, deepen your sexual energy. To know and express your deep being, it's best to curtail your spilling of attention into millimeter-deep puddles. Then you will have the strength necessary to penetrate through your old habits of body and mind, remaining vigilant and authentic to your deepest truth.

7 CURB FIDGETS

Fidgets are mini-ejaculations. Bypassing ejaculation won't be worth it unless you learn to conduct energy throughout your body with your breath. If you don't practice circulating your energy fully, then the built-up sexual pressure will just accumulate in various parts of your body, causing fidget, twitch, and fret. You will feel tense. Perhaps you will tap your fingers, bite your nails, or grind your jaw. Your increasing sexual energy will inevitably be expelled in restless movement as well as in random thinking.

Thought itself is often a kind of fidget, an unnecessary and random movement of energy, frequently serving no purpose but the expression of tension. If you develop the capacity for non-ejaculatory orgasm without also advancing your ability to circulate internal energy, this energy will simply build up in your body and mind. Your incessant thinking will only increase, your head dribbling with spent fragments of mull and agitation. Your head may ache and throb, too, with stuck energy of upward tension that you attempt to release via fidgeting and thinking.

It is important, therefore, to cultivate your capacity for non-ejaculatory living along with your capacity for non-ejaculatory orgasms. Practice relaxing the body consciously, especially when the symptoms of fidget and fuss begin to unconsciously puppeteer your extremities. Consciously breathe deeply and fully, allowing your belly and chest to be relaxed and open, your energy circulating in a deep current of ease rather than in swirling culs-de-sac of choppy thoughts and jagged fray.

Fidgets, both mental and physical, are the body's way of dispelling energy it can't circulate, exactly as ejaculations are. Both ejaculations and fidgets become addictive, so that you find it more and more difficult to stop the habit once the pattern has become ingrained. Your body becomes addicted to using fidgets, thinking, and ejaculation to superficially release tension, so it never develops the capacity to circulate energy deeply. Without this deep circulation, your entire life reflects a shallow disposition. Your creativity, awareness, and loving remain thin.

As a superior lover, practice redirecting the energy behind fidgets and ejaculations as we have outlined earlier—through your breath, contraction of the pelvic floor, bodily relaxation, and deep feeling—if you want to live as mighty, wide, and profound as you truly are.

8 GOOD EJACULATIONS LIBERATE ENERGY

I had a rough day. I felt agitated, tense, cranky. I ate a large dinner and felt stuffed. Then I got in bed with my lover and she started pumping my penis with her hand.

Within about two minutes, I felt like I wanted to come. I felt like I was going to burst any second. The pressure was entirely within my genitals; I didn't feel any energy moving through the rest of my body, and I didn't feel like taking the time to breathe more consciously to circulate the energy. I just wanted to come. I just wanted relief. I wanted to spurt my seed and get it over with and feel relaxed and go to sleep.

So I ejaculated. It was all over in a few seconds. I did feel somewhat relieved and less tense. But there was no depth to it. I felt emptied—which felt better than being full of stress. I was more comfortable. Soon I dozed off.

I woke up in the morning feeling fine. My first thoughts were about what I needed to do that day, my schedule and responsibilities. I wanted a little extra get-up-and-go, so I had some coffee before heading out the door. The day was OK, but I realized that it had not been the right time for me to ejaculate. I felt the subtle sense of inner ambiguity or lack of depth that I know can be exacerbated by inappropriate ejaculations.

A few months later, I again felt as if there was too much energy inside me. I had had sex for many weeks without ejaculating, doing my best to circulate the energy. This time, I felt the specific kind of internal "heat" that signals it is probably time for my body to ejaculate.

This time, while making love, I felt no tense need to ejaculate. My heart was not closed. My genitals were not about to burst. My internal energy circuit was open and flowing without obstruction. My entire body simply felt overabundant with energy, as if I needed to drain a little off the top so as not to overflow. This feeling had gradually accumulated over several weeks of steady vitality and strength. My genitals were not on the verge of popping as we made love, though I felt full of energy.

As our sexing continued for an hour or more, our energy rose and fell in waves, slowly and rhythmically, with a pulse of several minutes. My energy had merged with my lover's.

At times the pleasure was almost more than we could take. She would be screaming, crying, gasping, scratching my back and hitting me with her fists, while jets of light burst upward through our spines into the stratosphere of moveless awe. Then there were times of fecund love, heavy, thick, stock-still: two pot-bellied pigs swooned in the fat relaxation of utter trust.

Eventually, we both felt it was a good time to bring our cycle of loving to completion. I chose to ejaculate.

As the foothills of my ejaculation approached, I consciously relaxed my body, especially my genitals, belly, and chest. My face remained relaxed and my eyes open. I looked into the eyes of my lover as the orgasm energy built toward a peak.

As my ejaculation began, I relaxed into it. I opened out through it. It was as if my body had become water, and this water was enlarging, soaking my lover, filling her, the room, and beyond. I opened out and gave myself through this water, surrendering completely outward, holding no center or self.

Totally relaxing my body, breathing fully, looking into my lover's eyes, feeling into and through her from my heart, I gave her my love, offering myself to her, through her to depth's endless yawn. As I ejaculated, my whole body gave love like large water. My heart expanded to coincide with the water's expanding edge of love. A rush of oneness deliquesced my body in its giving.

Nothing was depleted by the ejaculation. I experienced no weakness. We held each other and breathed thick love. The depth engendered through our sexual practice continued into the dark of night, even throughout our sleep.

When morning came, the sounds and textures of waking life danced lightly in this depth. Our first impulses arose not in response to the schedule for the day, but from this well of being. As the day proceeded, our actions grew spontaneously from the smile deep in our belly, from the unencumbered curve of basic love.

●   ●   ●

Ejaculating too frequently doesn't necessarily make you feel bad, just mediocre. When a man has a proper ejaculative orgasm—when he truly needs one, and when he can relax into it and through it, yielding himself into and as love—then he and his partner are filled with energy and love, rather than depleted.

Ejaculating when you truly need to deepens your sleeping and waking. The river of your life flows with thick love and heart purpose, not thin coffee or scheduled need. Both you and your lover benefit from appropriate ejaculative orgasms, engaged at the right time and in the right way.

Men and women alike have a tendency to tighten their bodies, hold their breath, and turn their attention inward toward their own sensations during orgasm. Instead, try to relax, breathe, and open out while the energy surges. Continue to relax into and through your orgasm; don't tighten into spasm-then-release. You may be habituated to holding your breath and tensing your body in order to explode into orgasm. Instead, open your breath and relax. Continuously open out through your orgasm, whether ejaculative or non-ejaculative. Let your openness and love be communicated throughout the entire orgasm.

The moment of orgasm, like the moment of death, provides you a unique opportunity to discover the truth of your essential being: what remains when every shred of holding has been surrendered. Ease widely beyond form. Use the rush of orgasm to excavate all distance. If you are going to come, come like the stars in the endless sky, not like a balloon on a stick.

To the untrained lover, ejaculation seems like an all-or-nothing affair. However, when you learn to relax rather than become tense during ejaculation, and when you learn to feel outward through sex rather than go into the cage of your own sensations, then you can develop complete regulatory control over how big your ejaculation is, from a few drops to a thimbleful to a colossal geyser.

In general, the amount of semen you release corresponds to the amount of energy you release. By regulating the size of your ejaculation, you can better balance yourself, releasing only the amount of energy you need to release in order to attain internal equilibrium.

With practice, you will discover that you can explode huge gobs of semen and expend huge energy in doing so. Or you can seep a small sample, a quarter of a teaspoon or less, and not even lose your erection. Once a month or so (or whatever you discover to be your optimum frequency), you will be able to ejaculate just the amount you need in order to balance your internal energy.

At first, this control will be deliberate. You will predetermine how much you should ejaculate to achieve internal balance without depletion. Eventually, however, your body's inherent intelligence will come to the fore. Without any mental intentionality, your body will "know" how much to ejaculate. When you practice relaxing your body and breathing fully as ejaculation approaches, your body's intelligence will automatically determine the correct amount to ejaculate in order to maintain fullness and achieve internal equilibrium.

Your lover can probably feel the energy transmitted by your ejaculation. In fact, your lover may occasionally crave your ejaculation since it transmits a certain quality of energy that non-ejaculatory orgasms don't convey—although non-ejaculatory orgasms transmit a quality of energy that is, in general, much more subtle, profound, and powerful than that of ejaculatory orgasms.

If your lover wants to feel the energy transmitted through your ejaculation, the most direct way to receive this energy is through physical and energetic absorption of your semen through the lining of your lover's mouth, anus, or vagina (assuming, of course, that you have taken appropriate birth control into account). Even ejaculating onto the skin of your lover's body allows for more absorption of energy than if you were to ejaculate onto the bedsheets.

By choosing the amount of each ejaculation wisely, and eventually letting your body develop the natural intelligence to do so, you will neither deplete yourself through excess release nor suppress your body's natural liberation of surplus sexual energy.

Your occasional ejaculation can become a way to optimize and balance your energy as well as your partner's.

9 OPTIMIZE EJACULATIONS TO MAXIMIZE LIFE'S DEPTH

Learn to become sensitive to the signs of energy in your body and mind. Unless you are ill, of advanced age, or coping with intense stress, you should generally feel replete with energy and yet relaxed. Your breath should be full and deep. Your entire body should feel filled with vital force and ease, especially the major energy centers of your genitals, belly, chest, and head. Impotence, frigidity, promiscuity, lack of motivation, workaholism, ulcers, heartburn, heart disturbances, shallow breath, and headaches can all be signs of blocked energy in these major energy centers.

After you have opened your internal blocks and broken your addiction to frequent ejaculations, your body will discover its own natural equilibrium. If you are ejaculating too frequently, this equilibrium will be disturbed and you will feel tired, weak, depressed, unclear, and unmotivated. A man who ejaculates too frequently often finds himself addicted to stimulants such as coffee, cigarettes, or pornography. Even the stress of his career or profession may function something like a stimulant, compensating for his spent internal energy.

A too-frequent ejaculator may find himself unable to muster the energy to meet creative challenges and cut through the obstructions that arise in a creative life, so he may settle for a rote job, something he can do without really living fully. His financial, creative, and spiritual endeavors may be decent, but they will evidence far less expansiveness than he is truly capable of. If he has depleted his natural energy through excess ejaculation, he may find that all he can do at the end of a day is sit in front of a TV and zone out.

Alternatively, a man who doesn't ejaculate frequently enough may become overly picky, angry, and obsessed. He may suppress his natural flow of energy in other ways, too, becoming prone to fanaticism or zealotry, righteously devoting himself to a special diet, religious belief, or social cause. If he builds up internal energy but isn't sensitive enough to know when he needs to ejaculate, then he may also be too insensitive to properly circulate his building energy, resulting in "blue balls" or genital discomfort, as well as headaches, backaches, or emotional rigidity.

When you are ejaculating at your proper frequency, your energy is full yet smooth. Your mind is rested and calm, yet alert and responsive. Your creativity flows freely and you are able to meet difficult situations with fresh perspectives and great persistence. Your humor is quick and flexible, neither uptight nor excessively sarcastic. Your body flows with its full natural energy, and thus you tend toward optimum health for your age, constitution, and genetic characteristics.

Most important, you have the energy to grow in awareness. Spiritual growth — the deepening capacity to love through all situations and feel the infinite here and now — depends on having enough free energy to apply to the spiritual process. If you are squirting out too much energy in ejaculations, you just won't have enough vigor to witness the expanse of the moment; rather, you will get caught in its maze of transient forms. Hours will go by and suddenly you will realize you have been totally lost in a sequence of one detail after another, without even a moment of true humor or profound love to awaken your heart to deep surrender and clear recognition of natural and open being.

Nothing you do, nothing you *can* do, makes any difference to your deepest being. This moment of experience evaporates as quickly as you do it. Your lifetime flies by. In your death, how important will you find the hours you have spent so seriously entangled in dramas of money, sex, family, and knowledge? It will all be gone. Even now, the moments that seemed so important yesterday or ten years ago — the events that made you cry, scream, laugh, or rejoice — are now barely remembered in the present stream of assumed importance.

And yet, life consists of actions taken in this present moment: earn a living, take out the garbage, diaper your baby, read a book. Spiritual growth involves being able to take these actions — impeccably — while at the same time feeling through them as they arise in the midst of infinity. Then, you can have humor about your situation. You can live as love. As good or bad as this moment is, you can feel its transience, as well as the depth of primordial awareness in which this moment always abides. This recognition isn't a trick of thought or a philosophy to believe in. It is realized, or not, with your whole being, in the smack of this moment. *Either you are living as love or you are lost in the drama of your own story to one degree or another.*

One of the main effects of too-frequent ejaculations is a very subtle spiritual dullness, in which the scope of your attention becomes whittled down to the routines of life. This can be very depressing indeed. Being lost in the plot of your life — its actual routines — does not and cannot truly fulfill you. No matter how good your life seems for the moment, you will also feel like you are missing something, unless you are feeling into this moment's true depth.

Excessive ejaculation can dull you to the infinite depth of being in this and every moment. Cut off from your true inspiration — the love that is alive at your core — you can forget who you really are and get carried along on the river of things that you do. No longer sensitive with each breath to the deep divine, you may mistakenly look for spiritual depth and meaning in the surface adventure of your life—religious searches, social activism, family, career, relationships, drugs—rather than relaxing through your autobiographical saga into the ever-present openness of awareness and love, into who you really are.

Excessive ejaculation is not the only cause of this dullness, of course; moment-to-moment depth of awareness is easy to lose even under conditions of optimal energy. Sexual misuse of energy is just one important factor that contributes to spiritual dullness.

If you are an excessive ejaculator, you will rarely have the energy it takes to sustain the awareness you need in order to feel into the depth of this present moment and live as love, giving your deepest gifts. Instead, you will feel cut off from the effulgence of energy that is the nature of being itself, because all you can feel are the tasks in front of you. Since most men these days are excessive ejaculators, weakened and dulled in a subtle way, they are living lives of less depth than they are capable of. Most men can feel the lack in their lives. And they suffer it.

Thus, the best measure for frequency of ejaculation is your depth of awareness, moment to moment. Are you able to love through the events of this moment, feeling into the openness of awareness? Or are you lost in the unending details of the day, riveted to events, defined by the narrow mechanics of your attention? The capacity to remain wide in love depends on a subtle recognition of the depth and openness of this moment, which in turn is sustained by practice. You'll have neither the energy nor the attention to give to this practice if you ejaculate too frequently—or if your sexual energy is blocked in other ways.

In the way of the superior lover, you have sex as often as you like, but you circulate your energy rather than needlessly spending it in excessive ejaculation. You allow your increased energy to loosen your internal blocks by practicing full breathing, loving, and feeling, during sex and throughout the day.

Don't assume that your energy or consciousness is limited. Rather, relax and intentionally open yourself out into the space around you. As if you were pressing love into your lover, practice pressing your consciousness into the room with your breath. Embrace the events of the moment with your open love. Through the events of this moment, receive energy into your heart as you would receive delight from your lover's body.

Meld through any stress or sense of separation with a heart of trust, moment by moment by moment, so that relaxed and easeful oneness is your constant practice and natural home. Then, when your body needs to, when you can feel that it would be healthy for you—and not simply a spasm of addicted need—then and only then ejaculate, with as much love and open giving as you will allow yourself. In this manner, find the best frequency for your ejaculations, whether once a day or once a year.

10 EJACULATE WHEN THE BODY NEEDS TO

Non-ejaculatory, energy-circulating sex recharges your body with life force. Excess ejaculations weaken and deplete you. So, how much is "excessive"? How frequently should you ejaculate? There is no single answer to this question, since many factors influence your natural cycle of ejaculation. Your age, your diet, your lifestyle, the type of work you do, and even the weather all play an important part in determining how frequently you should engage in ejaculatory, rather than non-ejaculatory, sex.

To determine how frequently you should ejaculate, you'll first need to erase the old habit patterns of your body so you can feel its authentic and natural rhythms of energy flow. In other words, you'll need to break your addiction to frequent ejaculations before you can trust your body's messages.

To understand this better, let's look for a moment at the common addiction to caffeine. If you have been drinking coffee every day for years and then you suddenly stop, you might experience headaches, tiredness, and discomfort. Your body would seem to be telling you that it's bad to stop drinking coffee. But this would just be your addiction speaking. Your body has become habituated to caffeine, and it takes a while to get beyond this addiction. After about a week, though, your cravings for caffeine will diminish. It is only then, after you have broken your addiction, that you can feel what your body truly needs and therefore determine when to drink coffee and how much is good for you. Otherwise, you will be confused by the false symptoms of craving driven by the momentum of your addiction.

The same is true for your addiction to ejaculation. You must break your old habits before you can determine your best frequency for ejaculation. To break your addiction to ejaculation, you'll first need to practice the techniques of conducting energy through your body, up your spine and down your front, as we have discussed. You'll need to practice breathing, relaxing, and loving fully during sex and throughout the day. Otherwise, the tension you develop from a day of partial breathing and constrained loving will want to be released in an ejaculative spasm.

It may take several months of this kind of practice, during sex and throughout the day, before you can easefully bypass ejaculation on a regular basis. Once you reach this capacity, however, your inner energy quotient will increase day by day. Every time you have sex, circulating and magnifying your energy rather than throwing it off, you will be increasing your internal energy. And even though your internal energy is growing daily, you will be able to remain full and relaxed, breathing energy throughout your complete internal circuitry while practicing love and open awareness.

Age plays a large part in determining the most healthful frequency for ejaculation. Teenagers might ejaculate quite frequently without noticing a significant depletion of their overall energy and clarity. A man in his mid-twenties might ejaculate once a week or more and still maintain full energy and clarity. However, by the time a man reaches his late thirties, he will probably find it to his great benefit to ejaculate only about once a month. These are only rough estimations; each man needs to experiment to discover his own natural ejaculatory cycle.

As a man ages, it is natural for his ejaculatory needs to decline, and it becomes more and more important for older men to retain and magnify their internal energy. A man in his late sixties, for instance, may find it best to avoid ejaculation altogether, or at least ejaculate very infrequently — perhaps three or four times a year — if he wants to maintain optimal health, vigor, mental acuity, and spiritual depth. Every man is unique, however, and so each man must experiment to determine his own best frequency of ejaculation.

Diet and exercise often affect your circulation of internal energy and therefore influence your need to ejaculate. Excess sugar in your diet may make it more difficult to smoothly circulate your internal energy. Excess consumption of salt, eggs, and meat may increase your urge for ejaculation.

On the other hand, some of these same foods can also help revitalize you if you find yourself depleted from excess ejaculation. The foods that work best to revitalize you depend on your body type, metabolism, constitution, and everyday diet.

For many people, eggs are a powerful revitalizer after excess ejaculation. In fact, eggs are often considered a normal breakfast food among many people who are addicted to frequent ejaculations.

Depending on your regular diet, there are other foods that are effective for rebalancing your system after a period of excess ejaculation. If you eat a vegetarian diet without any meat, eggs, or milk products, then almonds are an excellent post-ejaculative replenisher. If, however, you eat a heavier diet, already rich in eggs and other proteins, then you may need something like a steak to replenish your depleted system.

Just remember that this dietary influence works in reverse, too. In general, the more eggs or meat you eat, the more likely you are to feel you *need* to ejaculate frequently. So, for instance, eating eggs every morning may make you feel the need for frequent ejaculation, as well as be an unconscious way to attempt to replenish the lack you've created by excess ejaculation.

Regular physical exercise—especially gentle and conscious exercise like yoga, tai chi, and walking—often helps you to conduct the energy circulating through your body, making your sexual practices much easier.

Your health and work need to be taken into account when determining how often to ejaculate. You should almost never ejaculate when you are feeling really sick or unusually weak. If your daily work is exceptionally strenuous—or you are simply exhausted at the end of long day—it is usually best not to further deplete yourself through ejaculation. When you are feeling tired or weakened, it is far better to have sex and circulate your energy without ejaculating in order to magnify your internal energy and strength.

How often you have non-ejaculatory sex also affects your need to ejaculate. For example, if you are enjoying one non-ejaculatory orgasm every day, you will naturally build more internal energy—and thus be more able to replenish energy spent in an occasional genital ejaculation—than if you are enjoying only one non-ejaculatory orgasm every month.

Weather plays an important role in determining how often you should ejaculate. In cold weather, your body needs to use more of its internal energy to produce heat, so you should ejaculate less frequently in order to conserve and build up internal energy. In hot weather—for instance, when you are on vacation in the tropics—your body doesn't need to use extra energy to heat itself, so your internal energy builds up more readily than in cold climates, and ejaculations will have a less deleterious effect.

Your body is something like a battery. Its store of energy is drained by too-frequent ejaculation, along with cold weather, excessively strenuous or unenjoyable work, disease, poor diet, and chronic tension. It is recharged with energy through non-ejaculative, energy-circulating sex, deep loving, appropriate diet, exercise, engaging in work you enjoy, and full and relaxed breathing.

After you break your old ejaculation habit and learn how to have internal non-ejaculatory orgasms, use the guidelines and effects described here to help you discover how often you truly need an ejaculatory orgasm in order to bring equilibrium and vitality to your body, mind, and spirit.

11 UNDERSTAND THE THREE TYPES OF WOMEN'S ORGASMS

Whereas most men lose energy when they ejaculate, many women find that when they have orgasms their energy actually increases and flows more freely, helping their hearts to open more widely. However, just as men can learn to convert ejaculatory orgasms into internal rejuvenating orgasms, women can learn to bloom their orgasms into deeper and deeper openings of rejuvenating bliss.

To cultivate enlightened sex, it is helpful to know of at least three types of women's orgasms: clitoral, vaginal, and cervical. Most women and men know only of the clitoral orgasm, which is a relatively superficial pleasure, a shard of trembling quickness. Without intimate knowledge of vaginal and cervical orgasms, many women remain unsatisfied, without ever knowing why. This dissatisfaction may extend far beyond the sexual occasion. A woman may feel something missing in her heart. She may feel an emptiness, a yearning that her man doesn't seem able to touch, try though he might.

Without the deeper invasions of vaginal and cervical orgasms, a woman's body may never feel fully ravished by a man's love penetrating into the heart of her being. She may feel his attempts at love. She may feel his care and affection. But her depth awaits the bloom of fullness.

In her unfulfilled longing, a woman may darkly dream of deep penetration by other men, bikers and pirates, horses and fantastic creatures, or perhaps an indefinable force that "fucks" her like no man ever has. And all of this because she has not been able to receive her partner's deepest penetration of ravishing love — whether lesbian or heterosexual — in her body and heart with full trust.

For years, a woman may tolerate her lover's ineptitude or her own fear of opening completely. Over time, since it's better than nothing, she acquiesces to rote sex. She settles for some lip and tongue between her legs, a penis or dildo entering her for ten minutes of thrust and seizure, her lover's hairy pubic bone perhaps grinding her nub relentlessly. But it is never enough. No matter how many clitoral orgasms she has, as her lover drifts off to sleep she is left deeply untouched. Knowing there is more to sex than this. Yet not knowing how or what to do to get it.

Eventually, she may despair of ever getting it. She may begin to resent men, little men, stupid men. Or she may fault her own poor self, convinced it is she, not her partner, who lacks sexual worth. Either way, bitching about her partner or depressed about her own lack, she shows the symptoms of an unravished feminine essence.

Sometimes her sense of unravishment has nothing to do with orgasm. Sometimes it is solely a depth of heart that is missing. But sometimes the body yearns, too, and clitoral orgasms often won't do it. For many women, vaginal and cervical orgasms are the necessary physical door to a more complete emotional and spiritual reception of love.

Women vary widely in their orgasms. The so-called facts we discuss here — how long an orgasm takes, what it feels like, how it is created — are only very general approximations. Every woman is different. Some women come like rain. Other women never experience what they would call an orgasm and yet are perfectly healthy in body, profoundly open in heart, and deeply fulfilled in intimacy. Not all women need or even want orgasms.

Furthermore, each woman differs from day to day and moment to moment in her orgasmic responsiveness. Much depends on mood, trust, and the special texture of loving created by the unique chemistry between lovers. Taking these caveats into account—as well as the fact that I am a man and thus in no position to convey the subtleties (or even the not-so-subtleties!) of women's orgasms—please accept the approximations presented here as guidelines for your own exploration.

12 ENJOY CLITORAL ORGASMS

I lay on the bed while she sat on my belly. She began to move her hips so that her crotch rubbed up and down my torso. She was making love to my belly, humping my abdomen with wet abandon.

Her movements grew faster and faster. As I looked up at her, she was a beautiful sight. Her long hair swung back and forth, sometimes covering her entire face before she flung her head upward to look at the ceiling, groaning and snarling, tossing her mane as if she were savoring the fresh meat before her.

Her breasts swung heavily, almost bursting with the fullness of sweet love. Occasionally I would sit up and draw her nipples to my lips and teeth before lying down again to take her wildness against me and watch her pleasure grow.

She raised herself on her knees and focused her movements so as to maul her clitoris against the muscles of my belly, again and again, back and forth. Her movements became smaller and more rapid. Her face squinched up, her eyes closed, her breath quickened.

She was coming against me, her body tight, her breath strained and fast. Her throat constrained the whimpers and shrieks that cried to escape. Her eyes closed. Suddenly, her body froze still and taut. No breath.

Then she relaxed in a final curl of short pleasure.

•   •   •

Clamp down, tense up, hold breath, release. For women, clitoral orgasms are most like male ejaculative orgasms. Since most couples don't make love long enough, with enough emotional trust and spiritual openness, many women end up settling for clitoral orgasms, which are plenty enjoyable. It's just that if clitoral orgasms are all a woman knows, she is missing much of what orgasm can be.

Clitoral orgasms are the easiest of orgasms. They occur for many women after only ten or fifteen minutes of manual, oral, or penile stimulation, near, around, or directly over the clitoral area—as long as sufficient attention is given to the rest of her body, too.

A woman may have difficulty achieving clitoral orgasms through intercourse for an anatomical reason: her clitoris doesn't receive sufficient contact during normal genital sex. Her lover's penis slides right by without sufficient clitoral stimulation to produce an orgasm. Adapting to this common anatomical mismatch, a woman's lover has to be careful to orient his pelvis in just the right position relative to hers, allowing his pubic bone, or perhaps the shaft of his penis, to rub against her clitoral area.

This doesn't work for every woman. Although clitoral orgasms are usually the easiest to attain, arousing the clitoris to orgasm is not always a simple matter. For some women, a tongue licking or fingers stroking will provide sufficient clitoral excitation. For another woman, it may be a combination that rings her bells best: for instance, masturbating her own clitoral area while her lover plumbs her vaginal depths with penis or dildo.

When a woman approaches a clitoral orgasm, her body often becomes more tense. Her eyes close, her breath comes fast, and she may seem to be clamping down rather than opening out. An ever-widening expanse of oceanic pleasure may become reduced to a swollen nub and contractive ripples. A woman may become emotionally disconnected from her partner in the moment of clitoral orgasm, enclosing herself in her own sensations just as a man may do during ejaculation.

You don't have to be very emotionally open, or deeply in love, to enjoy a clitoral orgasm. In fact, many women experience them best with vibrators, alone, focused only on their own pleasure and sensation. As with a man's ejaculative orgasm, even purely mechanical stimulation, done the right way for the right length of time, can result in at least a perfunctory clitoral orgasm for many women. However, you do have to be relaxed enough or willing enough to experience such pleasure. If you are too closed down or resistant to allow intense pleasure to course through your body, no amount of stimulation will make you come.

The clitoral orgasm itself tends to be short-lived and defined: several seconds of ripples and intense pleasure that may be repeated, since many women can experience clitoral orgasms multiple times during a single sexual occasion. In the range of potential orgasms, clitoral orgasms are relatively easy, quick, and superficial, not often the kind of orgasm during which women feel the "earth shaking" or the heart cracking open into a new freshness of love. And, like most men's ejaculative orgasms, clitoral orgasms sometimes spend, rather than enhance, a woman's energy.

Clitoral orgasms are an essential flower in the garden of many women's sexual pleasure—and they can also loosen the soil in which more fruitful tendrils of love may grow. The first orgasmic step for many women is learning to freely enjoy clitoral orgasms. It's important that women and their lovers don't stop there, though, since there is much more to come.

13 DELIGHT IN VAGINAL ORGASMS

We kissed and held each other in bed for a long time. I ran my hands up her thighs and grasped her ass. My fingers found their way to the crack between her legs and felt her wetness. I took my hand from behind her and moved it onto her pubic mound, cupping it firmly. She moaned and smiled. She squeezed her legs tightly together and then opened them, placing her hand on mine, pushing my hand against her mound, pushing my fingers into her wetness.

When she felt open and very juicy, I slowly slid one, then two fingers into her vagina. I gently explored her velvety terrain, every part of her sex region, deep and shallow, to the left and right, front and back. After touching her throughout her softness and feeling her responses, I began to focus more on her G-spot, about two inches inside her vagina, at the front and center, just behind her pubic bone.

Her G-spot felt spongy, a little bit ridged, differently textured than the rest of her vagina. I began to stroke up and down across this area, moving my finger in a shape similar to the gesture for indicating "Come here."

Her breath deepened. She touched her breasts with her hands. I took her cue and massaged her breasts with my free hand while I continued to stroke inside her vagina. Occasionally, I would enter her more deeply with my fingers, reaching to touch near her cervix, the opening to her uterus at the far end of her vagina. At other times, I would bring my fingers to the outside of her vagina, gently pinching, kneading, and stroking the area around her clitoris, as well as her vaginal lips.

Before she could get bored or familiar with my touch, I would move to a different place or change the speed or pressure of my strokes. However, I always returned to her G-spot, as if repeating the chorus of a song played for her pleasure.

Every time I would return to her G-spot, I would stay a little longer, her breath becoming more full, before I would move to briefly massage the rest of her vagina, from cervix to clitoris and outer lips. With my other hand, I would stroke her neck, breasts, belly, ass, legs, and feet.

This went on for some time, perhaps twenty minutes or half an hour, until her orgasm began to swell, like a wave rolling in from a distant horizon. I continued to stroke her G-spot, moving to other areas of her vagina when it felt appropriate. Her arms opened on the bed straight out to her sides, as if she were lying on a cross. Each of her fingers spread wide and long like rays of the sun. Her back arched and her mouth opened. She seemed to be opening herself to receive pleasure and love more and more deeply in her body.

She began to make sounds. Long, deep, open sounds, sounds of surrender and relaxed joy. Her eyes were soft, vulnerable, and wide. Mouth open, sounds open, eyes open, belly open, hands open, she looked into my eyes and unfolded her pleasure in the thick cream of our trust while a single tear rolled down her face from the corner of her eye.

•　　•　　•

Vaginal or G-spot orgasms are deeper than clitoral orgasms. They take longer to occur, sometimes thirty or forty minutes. And they usually require stimulation of the G-spot, which may or may not happen with genital intercourse.

You will need to experiment with different sexual positions and different angles of the pelvis to find a way for the penis, finger, or dildo to come in contact with the right place in the vagina. Some women find that rear entry, or "doggie style," is the best sexual position for achieving G-spot or vaginal orgasms. Other women prefer the front-to-front position, with the man's penis angled in a way to hit the front wall of the vagina rather than slide past it without much contact.

What is the right place in the vagina to receive stimulation for a G-spot orgasm? That depends on the woman. Some women have a well-defined area— the "G-spot"—a few inches inside the vagina on the front or anterior wall. This area is sexually responsive in a unique way. The spongy tissue under this vaginal surface may become full with fluid as orgasm approaches. Some women feel like they have to urinate as the G-spot is stimulated. Some women actually ejaculate fluid from this area during the contractions of an orgasm.

Other women do not have a well-defined G-spot, but still enjoy deep vaginal orgasms, which are very different from clitoral orgasms. I am using the terms "G-spot orgasm" and "vaginal orgasm" to mean the same type of orgasm: more full than a clitoral orgasm, though, in general, not as profound as a cervical orgasm.

Whether or not you are a woman with a well-defined G-spot, your vaginal or G-spot orgasms will be more full, more emotional, slower, longer, and deeper than your clitoral orgasms. Your body and breath will open during a G-spot orgasm, rather than close down and become tense, as often occurs during a clitoral orgasm. Vaginal or G-spot orgasms involve your deep reception of pleasure and love into your open and surrendered body, heart, and breath, followed by waves of uninhibited emotional and physical unfolding, whereas clitoral orgasms often involve a "clamping down" in short and intense pleasure.

Because of the deep opening that takes place in G-spot or vaginal orgasms, they require a greater degree of trust and communion than do clitoral orgasms. Most women can achieve clitoral orgasms through manual masturbation, using a vibrator, or being with a lover who knows how to stimulate the clitoral region with finger, tongue, or penis. But vaginal orgasms typically occur only with a partner a woman really trusts and with whom she is willing to open herself in deep reception and surrendered unfolding. G-spot or vaginal orgasms are as much about blissful emotional reception, openness, and surrender as they are about physical ecstasy.

A woman will have difficulty experiencing G-spot or vaginal orgasms if she isn't relaxed and trusting with her sexual partner. And even then, for some women the G-spot area is very sensitive, even painful in response to touch. This can be a good sign, however, for it reveals the potential for responsiveness. Sensitivity or pain often indicates that a highly responsive vaginal area has closed down—perhaps due to past trauma or simple frustration—and so it is resistant to further stimulation.

It takes time, patience, and loving sensitivity to help open up an irritable, resistant, or traumatized G-spot. A good way to do this is for a woman's lover to gently massage the G-spot area with his or her fingers while listening to specific feedback. The woman receiving the massage should describe exactly how she wants to be touched: "Slower, lighter, barely touch it, now move away for a few seconds, OK, now harder, harder, faster, now slower . . ."

At first, some women will be able to handle only a few minutes of G-spot massage. But, eventually, it is best to work up to an hour or more. If you are receiving the massage, you may be surprised by the amount of emotional residue stored in your vaginal tissue. During G-spot massage, you may find yourself suddenly angry, frightened, or grieving for no apparent reason. If these emotions become too intense for you to continue, stop the massage and simply be present with your lover, sharing what you feel while you relax and breathe together, perhaps while you are held and given refuge in your lover's arms.

However, if possible, you should eventually return to the massage, whether in a few minutes or a few days. With practice, you will learn how to continue with the massage *through* the emotions that arise. While screaming, weeping, shouting, or groaning, practice remaining fully present, fully experiencing and metabolizing your arising emotions. As the emotions flow through you, continue to breathe and feel every sensation fully, relaxing layer after layer of resistance and closure as your lover continues to massage your G-spot area according to your moment-by-moment instructions.

You may need to receive this kind of massage every other day for a week or two. Or you may require several months of careful G-spot massage. It doesn't matter how long it takes. Be patient. Take your time. Go at your own pace and intensity. Eventually, however, your vagina will open to this kind of touch. Your G-spot will relax. The emotional scars from past experiences — everything from memories of childhood sexual abuse to the residue of insensitive ex-lovers — will gradually dissolve. Just remember to continue breathing, feeling, and relaxing during the G-spot massage as emotions and memories arise, move through your body and heart, and disappear, bit by bit.

Once the G-spot area is freed of chronic tension, the whole vagina will respond differently to internal stimulation. If the man is able to stay erect for thirty to forty minutes, and if the penis and vagina are both positioned so the appropriate contact is made, intercourse can regularly involve deep and emotional G-spot orgasms for most women.

A common pattern for many women is to experience a few clitoral orgasms and then a final, full G-spot or vaginal orgasm, which often signals the relaxed end of the sexual occasion. Some women enjoy experiencing clitoral stimulation and orgasm as preparation for a full-blown G-spot orgasm, whereas other women have no interest in or need for clitoral orgasm at all. Some women stop after one G-spot or vaginal orgasm, whereas others prefer to continue making love long after experiencing a G-spot or vaginal orgasm, perhaps enjoying multiple G-spot orgasms just as some women enjoy multiple clitoral orgasms.

It is sometimes easier for a man to learn to bring a woman to a G-spot or vaginal orgasm with his fingers before he tries with his penis. With his loving fingers, he can learn the internal terrain of his partner's vagina. He can learn the rhythm, depth of touch, and locations that most stimulate his partner's sexual energy. He can listen to her verbal feedback and use his fingers to orchestrate her energy into a profound openness of feeling and surrender. Then, when he uses his penis, he will have a much better sense of what to do.

No matter how perfect her lover's technique, a woman will not relax deeply enough to experience a G-spot orgasm unless she trusts and opens to her own sexual energy as well as her partner's. If she is afraid of being seen in the midst of profound pleasure, she will close down. If she is afraid of feeling or expressing too much emotion, she will close down. If her partner is insensitive and emotionally disconnected from her, she will hold herself back for lack of trust.

If she feels her partner is weak in his masculine direction in life—for instance, his financial or spiritual purpose is unclear—she won't open to receive him completely. She will guard her feminine core in a subtle gesture of emotional independence, preventing a deep reception of love into her deepest parts and constricting her own expression of unbridled pleasure, surrender, and love.

For a really deep orgasm, a woman must trust her own sexual process—including bodily and vocal expressions of tremendous pleasure and the dark chaos of uncovered emotions—as well as her partner's integrity and his ability to embrace her pleasure and emotions. It is usually this fear of opening, rather than any purely physiological closure, that most limits a woman's profundity of orgasmic experience. Growing from clitoral to G-spot or vaginal orgasms is an important step for most women as they practice enlightened sex.

14 SURRENDER IN THE BLISS OF CERVICAL ORGASMS

For almost a month, I massaged the inside of her vagina with my fingers three or four times a week. At first, I would caress her clitoral and G-spot areas, only occasionally going in deeper. But after some weeks of this, I began to focus on her cervical area.

"Ouch! Stop, that hurts!" she exclaimed as I barely touched near her cervix. I slowly withdrew my fingers from her opening, and massaged her thighs until her readiness spoke itself. "OK, try again," she said. So I entered her, careful to feel her, careful not to impose my push on her vulnerable flesh or heart. I touched her gently, slowly, until she asked for more.

Eventually, as she relaxed over the weeks, I began massaging the area around her cervix. I slid my fingers carefully inside her, after kissing and touching and holding her, and administered my loving to her deep insides. It was as if years of resentment were coiled beneath her cervical landscape, years of fast men, shallow men, men of good intent but fearful hearts. As I touched her, week after week, the layers of incomplete loving made their way to the surface. She shouted, hated, closed down, and pushed me away with the unwinding coils of her frustrated tolerance, which had been wound tight from years of unfulfilling sexual infiltration.

Over time, her cervix began to trust me. It would greet my fingers with a kiss, a cervical smooch. I massaged the areas around it, near it, and also directly at the cervical opening. I was able to, finally, palpate her cervix with repeated loving, as if I were rhythmically pressing a button to her secret treasure, waiting patiently for her hidden chambers to open and reveal their wealth.

And so she opened. After weeks of cautious de-stressing, she wanted me deep inside her, coaxing her cervix toward absolute surrender. I entered her with my finger and then my penis, stroking against her vaginal lips, across her clitoris, along her G-spot, but always and repeatedly meeting her cervix.

Finally, her deep vagina, her cervix, her uterus, her whole lower abdomen, begged for merger. Her cervix craved a oneness it had avoided for years. It had been jilted, and so it withdrew, numbing itself to love, transferring its responsive power to its more shallow clitoral cousin. But now her cervix was empowered beyond the wounds of heart and fears of mind. My lover, previously unable to surrender to her own power of love, found herself grasped by her cervix, drawn through the hole of her resistance, and opened wide into a magnificence of feminine immensity that unfolded her soul into unbounded awe.

As I used my finger and penis to coax her cervix into absolute intensity, she opened out into a trust of God beyond her normal face of doubt. After an hour of loving, spontaneous, varied, and relentless imploring, she was sucked through the hourglass of her cervical doorway, spread out into the yawning oh-my-god of nothing less than all, and made fresh as the heart beyond her hide of moods and needs.

Her cervical orgasms revealed to her the basis of her trust: the open all of love. No fear. No closure. No need of promise and transient safety. The energy of ocean rolled her hips. The storm of love thundered her desire. As woman, no demand loomed larger than her love. She had known this all along. Every man and moment of her life only hampered or beckoned her immensity. And now, unprotected and cervically unfolded into the open of absolute fullness, her body echoed pleasure and abundance at every level.

Peals and weeps, oh's and confessions of unspoken love filled the space of our coupling. Her cervix dipping inward, sucking at the tip of my penis like a delicate bird of thirst, now growing into a great winged predator of fear. If I was holding back or less than true, she would feel me. Her surrender demanded my entirety. Her cervical orgasm rendered all meager attempted gestures moot.

Beneath her tears and crazed surrender in love, a wideness beyond all body swallowed this moment's spread. Gone in love. Gone in huge sex. Gone in the spacious oh of pleasure. Naked and disappeared in her transparent waves of orgasmic endowment, we were alight as heavy love, her cervix opening out to brighten the moment's disappearance into the eternal deep.

· · ·

Many women have never experienced cervical orgasms. Those who have, never forget them. Women who have had one or two of these extraordinary, earthshaking sexual revelations often refer to them as "religious experiences."

Other women, who experience them regularly, realize that cervical orgasms are beautiful occurrences of openness and deep surrender, but nothing to fret about. With practice, they can be enjoyed as frequently as desired with a trusted partner. Quite a few women, as their practice of surrender deepens, are able to open their hearts and bodies so fully in love that they experience cervical orgasms by themselves, while dancing, singing, or sitting in meditation without any partner at all.

Eventually, the lust for great orgasms begins to shift. Once you have willful access to any particular experience—whether cosmic orgasms, ice cream, or divine visions—you become less needy. You become less obsessed with obtaining the experience. You may still enjoy it, or you may be bored with it, but either way, it's just an experience. It may be a beautiful experience, but it doesn't change your life in any fundamental way. The experience comes and goes, but unless you make use of it properly, you continue on as you were before.

Fundamental change occurs when you grow to a new level of love, bodily fullness, or stability as open awareness. No experience can actually cause such growth, although certain experiences can provide you with a glimpse, an immersion, a reminder. Then it is up to you to *practice* being love, receiving pleasure deeply into your body, offering love's bright and open surrender, over and over again, as you become more stable in feeling and relaxing as your natural, unbounded, deep being.

Becoming obsessed with repeating any experience, such as cervical orgasms—or eating, or meditative bliss—tends to degrade you. You become so fixed, narrow, and addicted that you often become less loving in the pursuit of your chosen obsession. So, it is important to remain loose and unfettered in each moment of practice, rather than bound to the goal of achieving a specific experience. Whatever is your present experience, you can recognize the spaciousness that allows it to be. You are this spaciousness, this awareness, this luminous and open love. *Deeper love and more spacious awareness is the best lesson you can get from any experience.*

Cervical orgasm is no exception. It is often one of the most profound physical, emotional, and sometimes even spiritual experiences of a woman's life, by which she gauges all future sexual experience. But in itself, it is merely an initiation into an openness that could pervade her everyday life. That is, the cervical orgasm could be used as a way of remembering the possibility of love, fullness, and openness inherent in every moment.

Once you experience a cervical orgasm, you may still enjoy clitoral orgasms, but they don't really compare with the depth and fullness you now know is possible. Even G-spot or vaginal orgasms don't provide the heartrending, body-blissing surrender into unbounded light and fullness afforded by cervical orgasms.

The revelation of a cervical orgasm tends to recontextualize the entire sexual act. Sex is no longer about genital pleasure or even emotional connection with your partner. Enlightened sex is about profound surrender and dissolution in bright oneness. The sexual occasion shifts away from the pointed pursuit of pleasure or even intimacy toward the relaxed practice of blissful openness—ultimately, to the degree of effortless, effulgent, and unbounded love, a love that transfigures the entire body and heart. And this transfiguration affects both partners equally, if they are willing to actively receive such open light deep within their unguarded bodies and hearts.

Cervical orgasms often require forty-five minutes or even an hour of sexual stimulation. Clitoral orgasms and G-spot stimulation may be used as a warm-up, but most of the stimulation should occur deep inside the vagina, near the cervix. Some women find this area of the vagina either without feeling or painful to the touch. In many cases, this cervical numbness or pain is due to emotional tension, sexual trauma, or years of poor lovemaking technique.

The same methods should be used to relax the cervical area that were described for relaxing the G-spot area. Use very gentle fingertip massage near and around the cervix, and occasionally on the cervical opening itself.

If you are receiving the massage, be sure to give your partner abundant verbal feedback about how to massage you. Sometimes you will want slow and gentle touch; at other times, more firm and thrustlike strokes. Sometimes you won't want to be touched at all.

Do your best to breathe through whatever emotional and physical sensations arise during the massage. For instance, if your partner is massaging near your cervix and you suddenly feel intense anger, don't automatically stop the massage. Rather, express your anger — verbally, through gestures and shouting, or by hitting pillows if you feel the need — while continuing to breathe and feel fully as the massage goes on.

Breath is a key to opening closed vaginal tissue. If you hold your breath while being massaged, you won't be able to release the tension stored in your vagina, nor will you be able to bring fresh energy to numb and deadened areas of your body. Always continue breathing — inhaling down the front of your body, filling your belly and genitals, and exhaling up your spine to complete the internal circuit of energy — while your vagina is being massaged (and, whenever it seems appropriate, throughout most sexual occasions).

Your breath may change frequently, sometimes being slow and deep, and other times more quick and shallow. But, in general, keep your breath full and relaxed, not tense. Allow your belly to rise and fall with your breath. Allow your jaw to be relaxed. Notice if you lock yourself into a repetitive breathing pattern; instead, keep the breath fresh and responsive to your feelings in every moment.

Eventually, your cervix and the surrounding area will become relaxed, responsive, and, in most cases, orgasmic. During sexual intercourse, your partner's penis will need to enter at the right angle, speed, and depth in order to stimulate your cervical area. Since no one position or style works for everyone, you should experiment and find the ways that work best for you. Once your cervical area has been relaxed through massage, then deep, firm, and gentle thrusts of the penis (or a dildo), over a period of forty-five minutes to an hour, will often result in a cervical orgasm.

However, it takes more than mechanical stimulation to enjoy a cervical orgasm. Cervical orgasms are even more dependent on emotional trust than G-spot orgasms. Cervical orgasms are co-incident with your deepest surrender. Yield yourself utterly into love, trusting love without any resistance, actively receiving the invasion of love deeply into your body, giving yourself without restraint to your partner, and, more important, giving yourself without inhibition *as* love. As your body opens in total trust, the force of love moves through you unimpeded. Your emotional surrender opens your body and soul to a huge power of love and life that flows through you and fills you and overflows in orgasmic plenitude.

It is quite natural to shed tears during and after a cervical orgasm, even if you don't particularly feel the need to weep. Is it joy? Is it love? The openness sweeps through you and whisks away all mind, leaving only a deep well of expanding fullness. The sense of being a separate self is inundated with an indescribably bright oneness, a luminous openness of devotional surrender, as if your only sense of self were infinite love opened outward to receive all, your body widening to include and be filled by the cosmos.

The effects of such an experience can reverberate through you for days. Your body flows with a delicious and powerful force of life. Your heart feels radiantly open, sensitive, and alive. Any sense of lack or emptiness in your life is replaced by the knowledge of love, the intuitive certainty of love, the cellular relaxation in love's glow.

In this way, cervical orgasms are baptisms of true surrender. They are bodily reminders of the profundity of your natural openness, if only you would choose to remember love, widen your awareness, relax your body, give yourself completely, and receive the available force of life deeply, down to your toes, with every breath.

To remain this open through the ups and downs of the day takes real practice. It is so easy to close in the face of difficulty, a busy schedule, and unloving relations at work or home. Cervical orgasms provide a deep *yes!* in the midst of all the no's of life. They can help you remember that life is about receiving and giving unbounded love. Anything less than remembering, breathing, and practicing this openness creates numbness and pain — in the vagina, heart, and soul.

15 CHOOSE WHEN TO ORGASM

She began coming while straddling me. Her body heaved and glistened. I felt her waves of love echo through my body, soothing my masculine go and push, dropping me into the open of love. Then she lay flat on top of me, still coming and coming, her breasts and belly a soft membrane of merger.

I could not believe her beauty. It was not an eye, lip, or curve that carried her beauty so much as the offering of her orgasm itself. Her pleasure was so vulnerable, her love so vast, her trust so graceful, I was overwhelmed. What could I do but yield myself in reverence, belly to belly and thigh to thigh?

My body was made transparent in the power of her love. I felt the hurried nothing of my daily toil thinned by her thick feminine glory. I was disappeared into her, consumed in her large love, only to find myself as ever, love without move or need, pervading her every cell and soul as she surrendered ever more deeply. As I permeated her heart forever, her orgasm loosed love more loudly, and again, what was left of me was drawn into, through, and beyond the inconceivable beauty of her fearless vulnerability and open love. Her orgasm was a flower, drawing me more deeply into her fragrance, until I was gone in shudders and soft petals, rested as the love that is our very color.

Another time, she was coming, yet seemed totally closed off. Her breath was tense, her jaw tight, her brow knitted. She rubbed her nub against me needily, like a bear scratching an itch against the bark of an unwitting tree. Afterward, she simply stopped. She was done and tired. No depth had been revealed, no openness unfolded. Her coil unwound against my friction and now it was over. Her heart remained alone as before. And our separateness stung the moment.

•　　•　　•

Sometimes a woman's orgasm fills her and her lover with energy. At other times, though, a woman's orgasm may deplete and weaken her, just as a man's ejaculative orgasm often does.

With practice, a woman can learn to distinguish, at the onset, orgasms that are going to magnify her energy and open her heart from those that are going to deplete and close her. When she feels an energy-depleting orgasm on the horizon, she can breathe her about-to-orgasm energy throughout her internal circuitry, up her spine and down her front in blessed fullness, bypassing the kind of orgasm that might weaken her.

She can enjoy as many of these energy-magnifying, love-opening orgasms as she likes. These rejuvenating orgasms may be clitoral, vaginal, or cervical—or a combination—varying from woman to woman and moment to moment. In any case, these orgasms of fullness are a tremendous gift to a woman and her lover, sanctifying the couple in an ocean of celestial refreshment while reawakening them as effortless, vast, and original love.

16 ALLOW ORGASMIC VARIATION

She was washing dishes at the kitchen sink. I walked up and hugged her from behind. She came.

She was sitting on top of me, straddling me, sexing me with dripping fervor, grinding, grinding, grinding, for almost an hour, exhausting me. She never came.

She was just waking from a night's sleep while I gently entered her. Within moments, she had several short, quick orgasms. We continued making love, and twenty minutes later she began a low gurgle of moaning love, coming like huge bubbles rising from a deep lake.

I spanked her once, hard, softly caressed her ass for a while, then spanked her again three times, and she came.

I sucked her breasts for ten minutes and she came.

I planned the evening with her perfectly. Candles. A bath. A long massage. I kissed her body up and down, the way she likes it. I entered her gently at first, and slowly built up the intensity of our loving. I expected her to come in buckets, but she just fell asleep.

We were making love. She wasn't moving at all or making any sounds. Suddenly, she began crying. I asked her why. She said she didn't know why she was crying, but she just had the deepest orgasm of her life. I couldn't tell.

We were kissing, fully clothed, and she came in shivers.

•　　　•　　　•

Some women can have cervical orgasms with a kiss, or with no physical contact at all. Other women experience only clitoral orgasms, no matter what sexual positions they use or how skillful and loving their partners are. Still other women may never have what they call an orgasm in their whole life, and yet are more sexually fulfilled than some women who have orgasms by the dozen. Many women need slowly increasing stimulation over a long period of time, while others need almost none. There are women who can have an orgasm just by intending it.

Women vary greatly in their orgasmic potential: each woman is different, and the same woman responds differently at different times. There is no single orgasmic response that can be called "healthy." A woman may be multi-orgasmic or non-orgasmic; if she is able to relax and trust her deep heart's wisdom while surrendering as radiant and natural openness, then she will be gone in love from toes to nose. Orgasm isn't necessary or even always desirable. But for some people, orgasm can become a matter of great concern.

Some women's bodies and emotions are completely open and full of love, yet they simply aren't the orgasmic type. They enjoy sex immensely and feel deeply fulfilled without orgasms.

Another woman may be capable and desirous of deep orgasms, but her emotional fears may prevent them from occurring. Because her natural flow of energy is blocked, she will feel frustrated and empty, as if something is missing from her love life.

There are many reasons why an otherwise orgasmic woman may not experience an orgasm. Perhaps she is exhausted from a day's work. Perhaps she has a physical condition — an infection or injury — that prevents her energy from circulating fully.

Very often, orgasms are blocked as the result of emotional resistance to surrender. If a woman doesn't trust her partner, then she won't let go completely. What makes a man (or masculine partner) trustable, sexually speaking? It is his strength and openness of consciousness and feeling. It is his capacity to remain fully present, aware, loving, passionate, sensitive, fierce, playful, and spontaneous while also assuredly bringing the sexual embrace toward ever-new ground and deeper communion.

If a man gets lost in his own sensations, a woman can't trust him. If a man is bulldozing toward an ejaculation, a woman can't trust him. If a man is afraid to take the sexual lead, or if he leads without remaining exquisitely sensitive to her needs, a woman can't trust him. She won't be able to let go completely and allow unbridled energy to rip through her corpuscles and sinews, opening her to God knows where.

On the other hand, a man may be very trustable and still his partner may be afraid to open. She may automatically resist masculine sexual energy because she was abused—sexually or emotionally—by masculine energy as a child, perhaps by a father, brother, or acquaintance.

Alternatively, her mother may have seemed weak, manipulative, or unhappy, not an ideal example of genuine feminine power. Consequently, as an adult she may not trust—and may even reject—her own deep feminine strength, the oceanic immensity of her love, and her untamed passion and fury, preferring instead to cling to her own masculine style of strength, control, and self-protection.

If she lacks trust in either father or mother energy, she may remain emotionally protective and closed. She may fearfully limit her capacity to receive masculine love deeply into her open body and heart, or she may mistrust the enormous power of her own feminine wisdom and energy. Either way, she will prevent her natural orgasmic fullness.

Active reception is an essential, but often resisted, gesture of sexuality. The masculine partner must learn to open and receive the energy — dark and light, wild and nurturing — of the feminine partner. Likewise, the feminine partner must consciously choose and actively open to receive deep masculine love-penetration into her deepest heart and body if she is to dissolve in the fullness of love's obliteration.

If the feminine partner is unconsciously protecting her heart from receiving deep and penetrative masculine love, then she will be unable to relax. She will hold herself subtly separate from her partner's love and from openness itself. This emotional contraction or fear of surrender prevents deeper orgasms. It sometimes prevents orgasms altogether. And it certainly prevents sexual heart-fulfillment, whether a woman has orgasms or not.

To allow full sexual pleasure to course through you, to allow yourself to be overwhelmed by unbearable pleasure, you must first trust pleasure itself, which means embracing both the masculine and feminine aspects of sexuality.

Fear of loss of control, fear of openness, fear of masculine penetration, fear of feminine immensity — all these forms of fear and more can prevent the fullness of your orgasmic response to love. Therefore, to really relax into your native orgasmic potential, practice clearing the possible obstructions in your body, breath, and emotions so you are able to fully surrender as your natural flow of energy and openness.

The way of the superior lover is to love. Actively. Enlightened sex uses creative and skillful means of breath, surrender, and energy to dissolve obstructions to your loving. Then you can relax more and more as natural openness and love. Eventually, or in any moment of full practice, you spontaneously live open as love, breathe as love, and move as love itself. In the face of this natural enormity of love, whether you orgasm or not hardly matters.

Part Three: Variations

I remember one of the many times I received instruction from a woman about the different ways to stimulate sexual energy.

I was about sixteen years old, sitting in my mother's station wagon with my girlfriend. I had picked her up after school and we had driven to the beach. We sat in the car. Watched the ocean. Accidentally touched arms a few times. The silence was excruciating. Over the last several months, we had had sex a few times and made out a few more times, but it was weeks since we had seen each other. Finally we were together, alone, in a car.

After great deliberation, I reached over and held her hand in mine. I could hear her breathe a single deep breath, a sigh, really. I felt better. Yes. Holding her hand was the right thing to do. I had no idea what to do next.

She must have felt my eager dumbness. She said, "Can I show you something I really like?"

"Sure," I said, relieved that maybe I would now know what to do with her.

She sat back in the car seat as if preparing herself for some huge, overwhelming treat. I thought maybe she was about to reveal a mysterious fondling technique that the girls talked about with great longing while they smoked cigarettes in the high school bathroom.

I was still in the driver's seat of the parked car, holding her hand. She looked into my eyes and raised her eyebrows as if to say, "Are you ready?"

She brought her right hand to hover over the inside of her left wrist. Then, ever so slowly and gently, she began stroking the entire length of the inside of her forearm, her fingertips barely touching her skin. From the inside of her wrist to the crook of her elbow, up and down, very, very slowly, she caressed herself.

Her eyes closed. Her pelvis started rocking. I felt useless. Stroking her own arm, she was eliciting more pleasure from herself than I had ever seemed able to arouse with all my manly ministrations on top of her, beneath her, or behind her.

She took my free hand in hers and guided it to her forearm. She glided my fingertips slowly over the softness of the inside of her arm. Up and down, up and down, barely touching her silken flesh. When I got the hang of it, she released my hand. I was on my own. I continued stroking her arm. She seemed to sink further back into the passenger seat, licking her lips, rocking her pelvis, moaning from her belly.

On the one hand, I felt greatly relieved. This was easy. I could do this. If this was all it took to drive her crazy with pleasure, my days of confusion were over. On the other hand, I felt more befuddled than ever. How the heck would I have ever figured out that I was supposed to stroke the inside of her forearm to turn her on? What if she had never told me her secret? What other secrets wasn't she telling me?

Eventually, after I stroked her arm for about five minutes, she couldn't stand it any more. She pulled my face toward her and landed a kiss, a very wet one, flat on to my lips. Kissing I knew how to do. I put my arms around her and returned her sloppy mouthing, licking my tongue against hers. She pulled away and sat back. I wasn't sure, but she seemed disappointed. I must have done something wrong. But what?

I assessed the moment. What did I do to turn her off? For once, she didn't have to say anything. I figured it out: I had gotten lost in the fervor of our kissing and stopped stroking her arm.

I immediately tried to rectify my mistake. I quickly began caressing the inside of her forearm with my fingertips, just like she had shown me. But it was over. It wasn't working. The space between us hung static with nothing.

I continued to stroke her arm just like she showed me, but she remained stone cold. Who could blame her? My caresses were mechanical, bereft of feeling or subtlety. But worse, I was hoping to please her, hoping I was doing it right. I was being a good little boy, hoping for mommy's approval. I thought I was giving my girlfriend what she wanted, but what she wanted was the very thing I denied her.

I was slow to learn what she really wanted from me sexually. A few weeks later, we were making out, rolling around on the bed for quite a long time. Finally, feverish and panting, with wet lips and slut eyes, she asked, "What do you want me to do?"

"Whatever you want to do," I answered her.

"I will do anything you want. Anything!" she answered, hungry and hot-breathed.

"Well, I want you to do what *you* want to do," I answered.

"Anything, I'll do anything. I want to please you," she pleaded, licking me all over, rubbing herself against me, waiting for my word of desire.

"Just be yourself. That's what pleases me," I answered, sure that she would appreciate my acceptance of her.

Instead, she rolled away, went to the bathroom, and slammed the door shut.

Both in the car and in the bed, she wanted to feel me "knowing" her, taking her to a new place of openness and pleasure. She wanted to transfer the lead to me, so she could let go of being in charge and fully surrender in the pleasure of love. But in the car, I got lost in the energy of her kiss, and she could no longer trust my consciousness, sensitivity, or bearing. And when she asked for my "command" in bed, I threw the choice of direction back on her, making her decide for herself what she wanted. But this was exactly *not* what she wanted.

Growing up, I was raised to treat boys and girls, men and women, equally. To me, that meant treating them the same. I simply had no idea that in intimacy, sameness is not sexy. It was a while until I learned that magnetic sexual polarity is based on the attractive play between masculine and feminine forces, which are equal in power, but also very *different*. Sex is the play of their differences, their push and pull, their interpenetration, union, and pleasurable unity. But a mushy soup of neutered sameness is not the basis for sexual play.

The masculine in each person sees the big picture and remembers its real purpose, and thus is able to direct where things are going. The feminine in each person is the force of life itself, moving through the body, the earth, the sea, and the wind. Revealing itself through sensual flow, it is the energetic force of nature and aliveness.

My girlfriend had wanted to relax in her feminine, surrendering to love, allowing love's wild light to dance her body wide open, enjoying the delicious flow of energy moving between our hearts. Sometimes she grew tired of being in her masculine, always directing me. Sometimes she wanted me to take the rudder so she could flow freely as the wind and waves, undulating in sensual pleasure, not having to concern herself with what to tell me to do next.

Sometimes she wanted to be ravished, to let go and trust that I would lead us beyond our limitations into a bliss of loving that exceeded anything she could tell me to do. Sometimes her feminine power had the opportunity to manifest most fully when I took the lead, allowing her the freedom to radiate love absolutely through every cell, without having to compromise her shine because I wasn't conscious enough to take us deeper in sexual loving.

Technique is nothing without the play between the forces of trustable masculine consciousness and untamed feminine energy. Whether gay or straight, unless two partners are willing to play in the *differences* between masculine and feminine, sexual polarity and attraction will disappear, even if they love each other.

Enlightened sex involves magnifying the attractive differences and distances between these two powers so they slingshot through one another in a blissful interpenetration, the "fuck" of eternal unity recognizing itself.

Either partner can play either side of the polarity, in same-sex and opposite-sex relationships. A woman may enjoy playing the masculine. A man may enjoy playing the feminine. Partners can alternate polarities every few minutes, or play one style of polarity most of the time. But if there isn't an attractive masculine-feminine difference between partners at times, then sexual polarity eventually becomes neutralized, and the various techniques for stimulation and pleasure become reduced to friendly, feel-good massage therapy. For some people, this is enough.

However, for most men and women, neutered stimulation is fine on occasion but not a substitute for full-blown sexual polarity in love. Most people want to be sexually aroused, ravished, and undone in the resplendent bliss of "Oh my God!"—whose effulgence is sourced in the loveplay of unbridled masculine and feminine forces.

The masculine-playing partner cultivates the capacity to give the gift of trustable, all-pervading presence, so his or her partner feels deeply entered, sensitively known, and blissfully ravished by the directional love-force of consciousness. The feminine partner cultivates the capacity to give the gift of untamed expressions of pleasure and devotional heart-yearning, so his or her partner feels irresistibly attracted beyond separate self into the radiant bliss of real love.

If the masculine partner's presence wavers, then the feminine partner loses trust, guards herself emotionally, and can't enjoy the bliss of opening her body and heart fully as the offering of feminine love.

If the feminine partner's radiance diminishes — so that body and heart close, ripples of pleasure decrease, and emotional expression becomes muted — then the masculine partner is stuck in the realm of head and tail, bereft of full-bodied, heart-given sensual energy, unattracted beyond his own self-controlled detachment or selfish stimulation.

Knowing a wide range of techniques for stimulation helps to expand the ways you play your masculine and feminine forces in intimacy. While stimulating sexual energy, practice to remain present with your partner, connected in love, allowing pleasure to flow freely throughout your *whole* body as well as your partner's. Learn the techniques that best serve to magnify energy and open the offering of love in your relationship, however unfamiliar a method may seem.

Don't do something just to get your partner's approval. Do it because it serves to open your bodies as love. While your sexual energies are aroused, practice to unguard your heart, gently but persistently, especially when you notice yourself closing down. In erotic play, learn to enjoy the force of masculine presence and the power of feminine radiance. And always combine whatever variations you learn with compassion, sensitivity, creativity, and spontaneity.

17 STIMULATE THE SEX PATHS

Although the genitals are often called the "sexual organs," enlightened sex requires the whole body. The genitals are the root organs of our sex, but they bloom up through the spine and whole body, including the belly, heart, and head. Many people have grown accustomed to limiting intense pleasure to the genitals, resulting in ejaculative and clitoral orgasms. The rest of the body—as well as the profundity of whole-body orgasms—is ignored.

The superior lover knows how to stimulate the sexual pathways throughout the body. These pathways are slightly different from person to person, and over time each person's needs change. The best way to discover these pathways is through experimentation. When you nibble your lover's earlobes, what happens to the rest of his body? Which parts of your lover's body seem to move with energy when you pull her hair or kiss her neck? What happens when your lover bends his or her legs and you hold your lover's feet in your hands while you make love? Be careful not to get into a rigid habit of always stimulating the same parts of your lover's body in the same way just because it seemed to work before.

Pay particular attention to the ears, lips, neck, nipples, belly, anus, perineum, hands, feet, and spine. Use rough and gentle touch, sharp and soft pinches, wet and dry friction, tickles, scratches, steady pressure, and sudden blows to awaken and circulate your lover's energy. Through creative and skillful means, coax your lover's energy to flow so fully that his or her heart opens as spacious surrender, offering love, shining without boundaries. This is enlightened sex. Genital contact may get the sexual energy moving, but unless you are also skillful at helping it circulate throughout the whole body, the energy will just build up and deplete itself in localized blips of ratchety release.

18 BITE, SLAP, AND PINCH TO MOVE STAGNANT ENERGY

During sex, the body's energy may become stagnant, heavy, or stuck. Biting, slapping, and pinching can be used to stimulate energy in the nervous system and rouse a listless or sluggish body into more energetic ecstasy. Sometimes a little bit of pain, skillfully and lovingly administered, can greatly increase pleasure. Use these means freely, with real love and careful sensitivity. These techniques are simply aspects of creative sexual loving and should be used equally by men and women.

To begin with, choose a single technique to practice with your partner—for example, biting. While making love, bite or nibble your partner gently on the neck or wherever you choose. Then ask for verbal feedback. Would your partner like your bite to be harder or softer? More teeth or more lips? Work toward discovering how, when, and where to apply a bite. You can't just gnaw randomly and get the desired result. You must carefully feel your partner's energy, and when you feel that it needs a boost, provide just the right bite, at the right time, in the right place.

Then your partner can practice biting you. Make sure to give feedback to let your partner know how his or her biting is affecting you. At first it is best to use words to give this feedback. Once you both understand each other's signals, sometimes a pleasurable moan—or a sharp yelp, "Ouch!"—is enough. In any case, make sure that the pain is "good" pain, in the sense that it deepens and quickens the energy flowing through your bodies.

Erotic slapping can be more difficult to learn. Because slapping is often associated with anger and the desire to hurt someone, many people inhibit their impulse to smack a lover during sex. Remember, there is a big difference between hitting someone in a way that deepens the ecstasy and hitting someone because you are angry and need to strike out. What we are exploring is cuffing someone in a way that jolts both of you to a new level of sexual participation, openness, and love.

Eventually, you may find that an occasional and lovingly administered gentle slap to the face—not to mention the ass or thigh—can surprisingly open the sexing to a new level of abandon and passion. Both men and women can learn to gently cuff each other, at first being very careful and waiting for feedback before trying again. This kind of smacking or spanking is an act of love, an erotic expression of passion, and a means to move energy to a new place. It is *not* about trying to hurt your lover, although the smack may indeed be somewhat painful, or at least startling. However, the pain can quickly be assimilated into greater passion, pleasure, and bodily energy if the smack is appropriately and skillfully given and received.

For biting, slapping, or pinching to work well, timing is very important. You must *feel* the energy moving or stagnating in your partner before you can know when and how to assist the energy. Sometimes a smack to the buttocks will unlock energy. At other times, pinching a leg, scratching the back, or nibbling your partner's neck can be the skillful means.

Feel your partner's blocks. Where is the rigidity? Where is the energy flow limited? Which parts of your partner's body are expressing passion fully, and which parts are inexpressive, dull, or lifelessly passive? Your partner can feel and discover the answers to these questions in you, too. Carefully administered bites, slaps, and pinches can be skillful means to unblock and magnify energy in the parts of the body that need to be awakened. A sudden bite, slap, or pinch can also arouse greater passion and emotional expression in a partner who is drifting, mechanical, or lodged in torpor. By learning to feel your partner's energy with great sensitivity, you will know intuitively when and how to open and move it.

19 MOVE ENERGY THROUGH THE LIPS, NIPPLES, AND GENITALS

The lips, nipples, and genitals are connected through an internal circuitry of energy. By lovingly and delicately using touch to stimulate and relax each of these three areas, you can increase the circulation of love-force through your partner's whole body. Don't focus on one of these areas too long, but feel all three simultaneously, regulating the energy flow between lips, nipples, and genitals by using hard and soft touch, biting, pinching, rubbing, skimming, tickling, licking, and kissing.

When making love with your partner, stop moving. Lie motionless with your genitals interlocked with your lover's, your fingers on one of your lover's nipples, and your lips hovering near your lover's lips. Feel all three of these areas as if they were connected to one another by an invisible line of energy. Thrust a few times with your genitals and then carefully pinch your lover's nipple while staying attuned to how your lover's energy is flowing. Pinch the nipple just hard enough that you can feel your lover's genitals responding. Then stop pinching and continue thrusting again.

In a minute or so, begin kissing your lover on the lips. Use your tongue to stimulate your lover's lips while pressing his or her lips against yours. With your lips and tongue, suck and knead your lover's upper lip. As you do this, feel a direct connection from your lover's lip to his or her genitals, through your lover's nipple.

Focus on the lips, nipples, and genitals in turn while stimulating all three areas simultaneously to some degree. Based on your moment-to-moment feeling of your lover's energy flow, choose which area to excite, the depth of stimulation, and the timing. If pinching your lover's nipple or kissing your lover's lips ends up decreasing energy or closing your lover down, then, of course, stop. Even when something is working well, don't repeat it too long or it will become irritating. Varying the location, depth, and intensity of stimulation, bring your lover's body to greater and greater degrees of ecstasy, until your lover can barely handle it.

Then, when your lover's energy is very full, bring your chest and belly against his or hers. Firmly press your body against your lover's, your chest and belly relaxed and soft. Breathe as if you are breathing your lover's breath, in synchrony and with great sensitivity. Use your breath to deepen and open your lover's breath. Press your heart tenderly against your lover's heart, feeling through your heart into your lover's, thus reminding your lover to feel from his or her heart into yours. Physical pleasure should never overshadow openness of heart. But if you can continue to help keep your lover's heart open, there is virtually no limit to the depth and fullness of energy you can evoke by skillfully caressing the energetically connected lips, nipples, and genitals.

20 STIMULATE THE ANUS

The anus is a potent source of energy arousal in both men and women. Most people find anal stimulation either very pleasurable or very painful, depending on their degree of relaxation. From the perspective of enlightened sex, the entire pelvic floor can be a place of sexual power, including the genitals, perineum, and anus.

The anus is an erogenous zone, capable of giving you great pleasure. But it is more than this. The anus is also a "launch pad" for energy moving up your spine. Although not completely necessary, anal stimulation can be an element in your repertoire of practices whereby you circulate magnified sexual energy up your spine and throughout your body to heal and rejuvenate yourself and your partner.

In addition to being a source of great energy, the anus is one of the places we tend to store residual tension. Some of us are chronically anxious and therefore become a "tight ass." Others are clamping the anus in constant, low-level fear. It is important for you to maintain the proper muscle tone, but chronic fear and tension are unnecessary.

The amount of fear and tension you are suppressing below awareness in your daily life is easy to discover. This tension is stored in key areas of the body, such as your jaw, your solar plexus, and your anus. A finger up the anus will give you a quick reading as to whether you are unconsciously holding on to fear and anxiety there!

Everybody has different hygiene standards, but it is prudent to wash with soap and water before and after engaging in any kind of anal stimulation. Furthermore, remember to wash whatever is inserted in the anus before putting it in the vagina.

It doesn't matter who goes first, but you and your partner can practice stimulating each other's anus, one at a time. Start by using your finger. Lubricate your finger and your partner's anus with saliva, vaginal fluids, or personal lubricant you can purchase at a pharmacy or sex shop. Gently massage the outer surface of your partner's anus with your finger. When the anus relaxes, insert the tip of your finger into the anus about half an inch. At this point, vibrate your finger slightly to help relax the anus. You can also massage the outer ring of the anus.

With your partner giving you constant verbal feedback, you can, over time, go deeper and deeper into the anus with your finger, massaging the walls of the anus as you go. Listen to your partner, stopping when he or she says to stop. Much emotional residue may be stored in the tissue you are massaging, so be patient and prepared for anything, from tears to anger to catatonia.

Some people are able to receive a whole finger during the first session, while others may need weeks or months of slow and patient anal massage to receive even a few inches.

Eventually, when both you and your partner have learned to give and receive love and stimulation through the anus, you can begin exploring the subtleties of working with anal energy. You may choose to experiment with various kinds of anal intercourse, carefully entering the anus with penis, dildo, or butt plug. In addition to anal intercourse, you can experiment with anal stimulation (with your finger, for instance) during genital intercourse.

The purpose of anal stimulation is to help relax the body, release emotional tension, and stimulate the energy of the pelvic floor. This energy can then be circulated fully, up the spine and down the front, throughout the body's internal circuitry. The anus should be stimulated only to the extent that it serves this flow of energy and openness of heart. If anal sex becomes the sole focus of sexuality, chances are you are dealing with an unresolved neurosis rather than a skillful use of energy stimulation.

For some people, anal stimulation will play only a small and very occasional part in their overall sexing. For others, anal stimulation will be a more frequent part of sexual play and practice. Measure the frequency and style of anal stimulation by its efficacy in opening internal energy knots, relaxing the entire body, and moving energy from the pelvic floor up the spine and throughout the whole body. Most importantly, measure anal sex by its capacity to prepare you and your partner to surrender more deeply in love, a love without boundaries.

21 DO THE FEET

Your feet influence your whole body. When your feet are tired, the rest of you feels tired. When your feet are massaged, your whole body feels massaged. When your feet are touched with erotic love, the rest of you also flows with such love.

Foot massage can be a regular part of your sexual play. By massaging your lover's feet, you will help his or her whole body relax and open. Your lover will be able to feel your love, as well as your skill as a lover, by the way in which you touch his or her feet. If you just press a foot like a piece of meat, your lover will feel your insensitivity. But if you touch your lover's feet as if they were directly connected to your lover's heart and genitals — which they are — your lover will feel your skill with sexual energy. Your lover will relax in the trust of your care and sensual expertise.

To give a basic foot massage, use your thumbs on the sole of your lover's foot. Massage gently at first, covering the entire bottom of the foot, as well as the toes. Eventually, increase the pressure so you are massaging quite firmly. Also massage the areas around the ankle and between the toes. Your lover can give you verbal feedback and let you know what feels good.

As you massage your lover's feet, feel the rest of his or her body. Look at how your lover moves in response to your ministrations. Feel the texture, rhythm, and depth of your lover's breath. Can you slowly coax your lover toward an orgasm simply by massaging his or her feet? Can you at least turn your lover on so much that he or she begins to quiver and beg for deep loving? Your lover can also do the same for you by massaging your feet.

The feet are very sensitive, both as receptors and as transmitters. You can use your feet as you would your lips or genitals, to circulate sexual love energy between you and your lover.

Try treating each other's feet as full-fledged sexual organs. Suck the toes, licking in between them. Gently nibble and bite the entire foot. Touch your lover's nipples with your feet. Let your lover masturbate with your foot, touching it to her clitoris or his penis, or perhaps inserting your toes into her vagina or wrapping both of your feet around his erection. You can also actively masturbate your partner this way with one or both feet.

Always feel the effects of your foot play. Don't impose some weird sexual play on your lover just because you think it's a neat idea. The feet can be fully incorporated into your sexual play, but only if you remain sensitive to the effects on you and your lover. The point is to open the energy flow in the body, from the tips of the toes all the way to the top of the head. Even during normal genital intercourse, your feet should feel alive, flexing and relaxing, occasionally transmitting love to your partner directly, feet to feet.

Only when the whole body is open to the flow of energy can love invade the heart so deeply that sex becomes a means of contemplative bliss. Maintain a fullness of energy and awareness throughout the whole body, from toes to head, at all times during sex. So often, we live from the waist up, or even from the neck up, disregarding our lower body. And yet our lower body connects us to the earth. The energies of life can flow up our body and help us open in communion with the force of love. Make love with your feet and work up from there, until your genitals are conducting energy, your belly is full, your heart is wide, and your head is opened like a fully blooming flower.

The circular flow up your spine and down your front eventually approaches a speed or intensity that begins to feel more like a column of light, a bright and clear central channel of energy and openness. Breathe the energy up the spine and down the front of your body through your internal circuitry, until you feel like a hollow bamboo tube of radiance from toes to head. As your breath and energy become more coherent, a motionless vertical intensity shines as clear light infinitely above and infinitely below. As your heart relaxes all bounds, this intensity widens to include all appearance, so that everything seems as it always has, except now you are the intensity of its appearance, a motionless vibrating bliss dancing brightly as all things.

22 THRUST BOTH DEEP AND SHALLOW

While making love, it is very important to feel the energetic effects of your genital movement. This is equally true for both men and women, gay and straight. In this section, we will use the example of a man's genital thrusts with a woman. As always, feel free to experiment, modifying and applying these techniques to other sexual situations.

Any man can pump his penis in a woman's vagina, feel pleasure, and ejaculate. A superior lover uses his genitals to open the energetic knots that bind his partner's energy and emotion. Then, when her body is wide open, he uses his thrusting to open her heart, to magnify love. It is a subtle matter, involving a wide range of pelvic and genital motion as well as a keen sensitivity to energy flow and the nuances of trust and love.

As a starting point, practice feeling the energetic differences between shallow and deep thrusting. Shallow thrusting means moving the head of your penis from your lover's vaginal opening to about three inches or so inside her vagina. Moving in and out at this shallow depth stimulates the clitoral area as well as her G-spot area. Furthermore, by denying her deep penetration, your shallow thrusting creates a desire in your lover for the energy of deep thrusts.

Deep thrusting means entering your lover as deeply as possible. For most men, this means that the head of the penis thrusts near her cervix. Besides stimulating cervical orgasms, deep thrusts allow your lover to feel profoundly penetrated by your love. This deep penetration of love—physically, emotionally, and spiritually—is the essence of the masculine sexual gift. If and when your lover is ready, you can enter her so deeply that she has no choice but to receive you utterly, surrendering and opening without limit as love.

Try different combinations of shallow and deep thrusts while making love. In general, especially near the beginning of a love-making occasion, shallow thrusts should outnumber deep thrusts. A good rule to follow while you are developing sensitivity is to use about nine shallow thrusts followed by one deep thrust. Once you can actually feel the currents of energy flowing between you and your partner, frequency and depth of thrusting become obvious and spontaneous matters.

While you are thrusting shallow, feel as if you are priming your lover's pump. Her desire to receive you deeply increases as she is stimulated superficially but denied deep penetration. Likewise, you may build up a desire to plunge in as deeply as possible and really pierce your woman to her core. By not succumbing immediately to these desires, you create an energetic vacuum that begins to suck you and your partner into the deepest giving possible, beyond what you would otherwise tend to give of yourselves. This combination of many shallow and a few deep thrusts also creates a physical vacuum inside your lover's vagina, producing a unique sensation alternating between suction or yearning (during shallow thrusts) and fullness or merger (during deep thrusts).

During the deep thrusts, visualize or feel your penis extending far beyond its actual physical length. As you enter deeply into your lover, it is as if the energy of your penis extends through her cervix, through her womb, up through her heart, and perhaps even up through the top of her head. Hold yourself deeply within her, feeling her loving reception of your love, while you remain motionless, yielding your sense of separation, giving yourself completely to your lover and through her, so that you are gone in the giving.

Your giving of love and penetration of her heart may become so complete that no sense of separation remains, for you or her. Feeling her completely, you are willingly giving yourself in love. You are pervading her body with your consciousness and energy, feeling through her, taking her beyond herself as both of you are undone in love.

When you enter her with your unrelentingly deep yet totally trustable force of love, she can practice surrendering fully—physically, emotionally, and spiritually. Her vagina opens in pleasure. Her heart widens in love. Her love-bliss unfolds in response to your conscious entrance into her deepest, most hidden chambers of love. To open so completely, she must feel the *trustable* force of your body, your love, and your consciousness. She must be *tenderly* and *deeply* penetrated by all three of your masculine sexual gifts—penis, heart, and consciousness—before she will fully reciprocate and offer you her most profound devotion and surrender.

As you practice over time, she will feel the strength, care, and persistence of your love as you yield your separate sense of self and enter her deepest parts in physical, emotional, and spiritual unity. She can open her vagina, heart, and soul with complete abandon, receiving the obliterating depth of your loving, and both of you will be blissfully vanished in sexual self-yielding.

In addition to helping you and your partner open in love, an assortment of thrusts can help magnify and circulate the sexual energy flowing between you. A variety of thrusts may include shallow and deep thrusts, but also churning, twisting, rotating, and vibrating styles of thrusting, as well as thrusts directed toward specific areas of her vagina. For example, following a deep thrust, it is sometimes very useful to vibrate deeply inside your partner, so that your penis is moving back and forth only a fraction of an inch, but at a very fast rate.

In order to determine what types of thrusts to use, feel your partner's energy. Is it rising deliciously up her spine, causing her back to arch? Is it descending fully down her front so her vagina is pulsing with power, squeezing, sucking, and churning? Or is there a deficiency of downward energy, robbing her vagina of life so that it feels slack and passive? Is there too much energy stuck in her head, causing her face to be tense and her legs to be empty? Is her pelvis moving smoothly with the flow of energy, or does it seem rigid, ratchety, or stuck? Are her belly and chest tight and resistive, or do they feel soft, open, and receptive, welcoming your body to melt into hers? Use whatever thrusts serve to open your lover more deeply, as well as to stimulate and circulate full life energy throughout her entire body and your own.

To choose the appropriate style of thrusting for the moment, consider your lover's capacity to receive love. If your lover is in a closed mood, feeling hurt and shut down, then you are not likely to elicit a great response from suddenly thrusting deeply within her. Instead, you will need to use only careful, gentle, shallow thrusts, slowly opening her, showing her you are trustable, and coaxing her heart to receive your loving more deeply. Only after a prolonged period of shallow and caring touches of love will she be ready for the full force of your loving, perhaps pressing into her cervical area.

The important point is not whether you should thrust shallow or deep, but whether you are skillfully circulating energy and opening yourself and your partner to deeper loving and awareness. In the fullness of love, no holds are barred. Until then, make sure your lover really wants you to thrust deeply before you cross any physical or emotional barriers that may not be ready to relax.

23 CONNECT THE CERVIX AND PENIS

Often, men ejaculate too quickly and women are unable to receive deep love-penetration. Thus, the clitoris has become the focus of some women's sexuality. But for many women, the cervix holds a key that unlocks the physical and emotional doors to truly spiritual sexual union.

If a couple's sexual organs are of compatible size, the head of a man's penis, when fully inserted, fits firmly against a woman's cervix. However, vaginas and penises vary in size from person to person, so couples may have less than perfect compatibility between their sex organs. For some couples, the penis might penetrate through the cervix into the uterus if the man thrusts hard enough. For other couples, the head of the penis falls short of the cervix no matter what position the couple takes during sex. Careful experimentation will teach most couples how to accommodate the size and shape of each other's genitals.

Couples often need to experiment with different sexual positions to find the best posture for penis-cervix contact. If the vagina is shorter than the penis, the woman and man may lie belly to belly during sexual intercourse, with the woman keeping her legs pressed together. This posture prevents the man from entering too deeply and painfully beyond the woman's cervix. If the vagina is longer than the penis, the woman may need to lie on her back and place her legs on the man's shoulders while they are facing each other in order for him to enter deeply enough to contact her cervix. For some couples, the "doggie-style" position, with the woman kneeling and the man entering her from behind, is the best position to use for cervical stimulation by the penis.

Pay attention to how you feel when the penis is in contact with the cervix. If the penis is motionless against the cervix for too long, the man may eventually begin to lose his erection and the woman may begin to feel less aroused. This is due not only to the lack of movement, but also to the equilibrating effect of the energy flowing between the cervix and the head of the penis.

Separate the penis and the cervix just a bit and feel the shift in energy. Practice feeling the difference between cervical contact and more shallow genital contact.

Build up a force of sexual energy by using shallow thrusting. Take care that the penis does not contact the cervix. When both partners are filled with sexual energy, then slowly but firmly move so that the head of the penis contacts the cervix. At first, do this with your eyes closed so you can more easily feel the effects. Eventually, keep your eyes open, gazing deeply into your partner's eyes.

Either partner can vibrate so the head of the penis and the cervix quiver against each other, increasing the flow of energy between partners. The hot masculine energy from the penis is received through the woman's cervix and moves up the woman's spine while her cooling feminine energy is received through the penis and moves up the man's spine. Then, before you feel depleted or bored, separate the penis and the cervix and continue with shallow thrusting, remembering to circulate energy through your complete internal circuitry, up the spine and down the front.

Couples can experiment with different styles of contact between penis and cervix: forceful, gentle, sharp, slow, repeated bumping, vibrations, just staying in place, or even penetrating through the cervix. Of course, any kind of cervical contact must be done with great care and sensitivity. At first, the woman should guide the man with her words. Remember that a woman's cervical area often stores the residue of old sexual and emotional traumas and stress, and, therefore, it may be quite painful for her when her cervix is penetrated or even gently touched by the tip of the penis. These old emotional stresses can be released as previously described before couples freely engage the energetic circulation and deep transmission of love through uninhibited penis-cervix union.

24 VIBRATE QUICKLY TO INCREASE AND SMOOTH OUT ENERGY

Many people limit their sexual motion to a few styles and speeds. Some of the more popular include gentle, fast and furious, aggressive, orgasmic, and calm. Although there are infinite numbers of potential motions during sex, one motion bears emphasizing. This is the vibrating motion.

Vibrating does not mean thrusting really fast. It is actually more like a bodily buzzing, like a vibrator. Imagine putting your hand on the hood of your car while the engine is running. This is what it feels like to vibrate during sex.

It takes time to learn how to vibrate your body. It is something like the motion of shivering, though you do it consciously during the heat of sexual embrace. Practice "shivering" with the muscles of your buttocks. This creates a vibrating motion in your pelvis.

This vibrating motion smoothes out your energy and your lover's, magnifying but also dispersing the energy. Rather than a building-up sensation, vibrating serves to enlarge and smooth out sexual energy. Vibrating should be used periodically during lovemaking, whenever the energy becomes too intense or one-pointed.

If you are a man, practice vibrating your pelvis against, and your penis inside, your lover. Vibrating usually works best when the head of your penis is against your lover's cervical area, but it is also useful when your penis is more shallowly placed, perhaps only a few inches into your lover's vagina.

If you are a woman, practice vibrating your pelvis while your lover is inside you, thus surrounding his penis with vibrations.

As long as he knows how to circulate his energy, your vibrations will serve to smooth out his energy if he has become too goal-oriented and one-pointed.

Men and women can also vibrate their whole bodies against one another, especially the belly and chest. If you feel that your lover is holding his or her breath or is too tense, simply stop your thrusting motions and lie firmly against your partner, belly to belly. Vibrate your open chest and soft belly against your partner's. Breathe deeply and steadily while you vibrate, never holding your breath. Feel your partner's energy loosen and open with your vibration.

When your partner's body feels soft and relaxed, like love-jelly, then you can resume other motions to increase and circulate energy. Throughout your lovemaking, allow your body to remain liquid and pliable, rather than rigid and stiff. Periodically, you can vibrate against your partner—just through your genitals or with your entire body—to help keep both of you soft, alive, and lovingly vibrant.

25 RELAX YOUR BODY AND BREATH

If you have ever seen a great athlete perform, then you have seen grace in motion. Great athletes remain deeply relaxed, even when they are very active. This combination of relaxed ease and skillful activity is the hallmark of bodily genius. The same quality of graceful fluidity can be found in great musicians, singers, and dancers, as well as basketball, baseball, and football players. Spiritually evolved individuals, such as saints and true mystics, often evidence a uniquely graceful economy of movement.

As your practice of enlightened sex develops, your movements become more and more like those of a great athlete, dancer, or saint. Rather than flail like a worm in a frying pan, you move more like the waves rolling across an ocean—powerful, serene, and vast. Your heart opens through your body and beyond, so every movement is generated by the force of love. Your belly and genitals are full of energy, and all action emanates from your energy-full lower belly. Your tempo of thrust and spine undulates with the rhythm of your inhalations and exhalations.

With practice, deep consciousness pervades every stirring of your belly, breath, and heart. It is as if your sexing is the play of ripples on the surface, but the deep ocean currents are its source. The deep of consciousness unfolds through your belly, breath, and heart, and this is enlightened sex: consciousness unfolding through the body as love.

Unless consciousness can pervade your body, love will not prevail. If your body is kinked by tension, the immense force moving through you cannot unfold as love. Rather, it will unfold in the shape of your kinks.

If you are afraid of anger, for instance, this fear will be shaped as a kink in your body. As sexual energy becomes magnified, it will echo in the shape of the kink. Your fear of anger will become greater. Your breath will become shallow and your body will tighten. Tension will increase and the flow of love will decrease. Because of energy echoing in the shape of your kink, you may automatically react to your partner's passionate or aggressive expression of lovemaking as if it were an angry violation of your boundaries, even when it is only a playful expression of love.

As we learn to open fully in the play of enlightened sexuality, we must remember to keep the body relaxed, so love can flow fully through all our parts. Tension causes love to kink into fear. Tension obstructs the energy magnified through sex, energy that would otherwise be used for transmitting love to our partner and beyond. The more relaxed our body remains, the more our sexual motions reflect the vast consciousness that is the source of our being. The more fully our breath circulates through our body, the more our love can unfold through every gyration and moan.

However, a relaxed body does not mean a limp body. An open body is not a passive body. Consider an athlete or dancer. He or she is very active, full of great force and dynamic energy. And yet, his or her movements are relaxed, at ease, and graceful. Over time, you can develop this capacity during sex, so you are simultaneously powerful and relaxed.

Pay special attention to keeping your body relaxed as the energy builds during lovemaking. If you notice your forehead crinkling, smooth it out. If you notice your jaw clenching, relax it. If your belly and chest become hardened, allow them to be soft and open. Keep your whole body fluid and alive. Allow your energy and power to move through you without clamping down the body.

Allow your power to be wide and round, rather than narrow and one-pointed. If your thrusting becomes rigid and knifelike, round it out into the form of a huge crashing wave. If your shrieks become sharp, open them into full-throated moans. If your limbs go stiff, move them with the slithering power of big snakes. Without decreasing the force of your energy, allow it to flow like huge water, rather than like a monster robot. Your strength can be that of a waterfall or a giant redwood tree, rather than that of a metal pole or concrete slab. You are alive and filled with energy, not dead and rigid.

Your breath fills your body with life force. Just as blowing into a balloon fills its limp rubbery skin with pressure, or as wind fills the sails of a huge ocean vessel, so your breath fills every inch of your body with energy. Your movements ride on this force of breath.

When you practice enlightened sex, the large movements of your pelvis and spine ride the rhythm of your inhalation and exhalation. And even your smaller movements—kissing your lover's neck, for instance—are done at the right moment of breath in order to transmit the most love. You must feel and learn what the right moment of breath is, and this is done by remaining aware of your breath and the flow of energy during lovemaking.

Imagine a place about two or three inches below your navel. This is your center of movement. Every movement of yours can feel connected to this place, as if the impulse to move even your fingertips emanated from this area in your lower belly. Move from your lower belly, and allow all motions to unfold as love through your breath.

If you are spreading your legs wider, for instance, allow this action to originate from your lower belly. Drop your attention and awareness to your belly, to your center of power and movement, two or three inches below your navel. Feel this area below your navel. Inhale and feel your belly rising with your breath, pushing outward. Feel your hips and upper thighs separating with this motion.

Widen your legs in synchrony with either your inhalation or your exhalation, whichever feels more open, natural, and easeful. Do the motion itself as an act of transmitting love to your partner. As if kissing a child, allow your action to communicate total love. As if massaging a stiff muscle, offer your motion with the conscious intent to open your partner even wider into love.

With practice, your body, breath, and heart will become synchronized with your partner's. A coherence will develop between the two of you, magnifying your life force and depth of loving beyond what you could manage alone. As you both relax through your kinks, fears, and resistances, love will pervade you to a profound degree, until your bodies become as waves in an immense ocean of love. The power of love will express itself naturally and spontaneously through your relaxed breath and body as the play of your sexing unfolds from greater and greater depths. The grace of your lovemaking may provide an opening through which eternity can flood its hello.

26 MAKE LOVE FOR AT LEAST FORTY-FIVE MINUTES

Sex is enjoyable in various portions. Sometimes you just want a quick dollop of passion during lunch hour. A brief ravishment in the car can move your energies and awaken your hearts for the remainder of the day. There are many times when a short sexual occasion is just what you and your partner need. However, sexual occasions of long duration can be the mainstay of your sexual practice.

As animals, our bodies are built for sex. Upon stimulation, we get hard and wet and want it more and more. We touch, couple, and gyrate like writhing mammals of love, finally convulsing in an orgasm. Our penis spews seed. Our cervix dimples and sucks sperm toward the waiting egg. This kind of sex is best for making babies. Two minutes or ten minutes, it really doesn't matter too much if our desire is to procreate.

But if our desire is to circulate healing energy through our bodies, loosen the tightened knots around our hearts, and surrender into open communion as love, then we can practice sex for longer periods of time.

Something happens to the energy of the body after about forty-five minutes of sexual intercourse. Our urgency smoothes out. Our tension eases into an open love. The wrinkles of the day flatten into a calm sea that washes through us in a bigger way than a normal orgasm ever could. For many people, the fullest sexual potential starts after about forty-five minutes of active loving.

For women especially, the sexual occasion is one of gradual heating to the boiling point. Deep cervical orgasms, for instance, typically don't emerge until after forty-five minutes or more of sex. And for many men, the urge to ejaculate is strongest after two to ten minutes of sex. If a man can continue making love without ejaculating for forty-five minutes, his body reaches a plateau of energy. He can then more easily sustain a high intensity of lovemaking for a long time, enjoying multiple, whole-body orgasms without ejaculating.

The knots of tension that obstruct energy and block the heart are usually not opened by a short sexual session. These knots often require the steady and persistent circulation of energy that only a longer session affords.

These very knots can sometimes keep us from long and leisurely sexual practice. Our sexual energy builds in our body as we make love. Then the knots act like dams, blocking our internal energy flow, forcing us to spill out our energy in ejaculations, hoots, hollers, and convulsions of tension and release.

If, instead of overflowing, we steadily practice to open the dams of our tension, then the knots can open. Our deep heart-energy can flow throughout our body. Relaxing as love's bright flow, our body is unbound from the force of fear that tied the knots to begin with.

Every time we experience fear or hurt during the day, we tie our internal knots a little tighter. Unless we are very conscious and learn to breathe and circulate energy throughout the day, we end up accumulating a remarkable storehouse of tension within our body. The stock market takes a plunge, and the fear of loss ties a knot within. Our child is late from school, and fear ties another knot around our heart. Our lover threatens to leave — or insists on marriage — and another knot of fear tightens through our gut and chest. Fear — along with the anger, worry, and grief that result from fear — is stored in every knot.

Mediocre lovers find it easier to spurt and shimmy away sexual energy than to open their internal knots, which would allow their energy to circulate in a much more profound and blissful depth. They can't sustain the practice of circulating love's energy through their knots. Why? Because to circulate love's energy, they would have to loosen their knots and, in doing so, release the fear stored within them, which often creates panic, nausea, or even moments of relived trauma. Mediocre lovers are afraid of letting go and *feeling*. They are afraid of feeling hurt, rejected, abandoned, taken advantage of, and ripped off; they are even afraid of feeling loved. To circulate energy freely throughout the body and heart requires that we feel, embrace, and open, loving our fears, moment to moment. Surrender is the texture of loving even while afraid.

Long sexual occasions are not simply a means to greater physical pleasure, although certainly the fathomless ecstasies that arise deep into a long session of loving far surpass the surface flash of an early orgasm. Beyond sheer enjoyment, sexual occasions of forty-five minutes or more are often necessary for opening the body and heart to the fullest potential of human love and intimate communion. Otherwise, the knots in our body and heart detour our loving into brief excursions of shallow pleasures.

As a practice for a month, try having at least one occasion per week of continuous sexual intercourse that lasts forty-five minutes or longer. Vary the depth, style, and position of sexing to allow the body to remain relaxed and open. Use the breathing techniques and upward tension of your pelvic floor (discussed earlier and explored fully in Part Four) to circulate the energy and bypass ejaculative or weakening orgasms.

Be wary of misinterpreting symptoms. Sometimes vaginal soreness or a lost erection are signs of emotional knots being tweaked. Don't assume that the only solution to discomfort or lack of interest is to stop having sex; instead, continue making love with sensitivity and care while circulating energy through your fears and tensions.

Do your best to make love while any and all emotions are fully felt and expressed. Don't be afraid to verbally express the strangest emotions. You might find yourself shouting "I hate you!", "Kill me!", "Fuck you!", or any number of emotionally charged and seemingly negative expressions. Feel fully whatever you are feeling and continue having sex, loving whatever emotions arise, while also feeling your partner's heart. Circulate your energy through any knots of tension you encounter, until the knot is loosened or thoroughly untied. Make sure that you and your partner have a way of communicating "Stop!" in the event that you reach a limit you are not yet ready to breathe and love through.

Eventually, after weeks or months of long lovemaking sessions in which you are practicing sex through all the knots you encounter, your body will be much more emotionally open. Your sexual energy will flow more fully and freely, without getting stuck in kinks. This free energy and emotional openness will help you to remain more fully conscious of your true depth of being, rather than be stopped short by the knots of your thoughts, fears, and desires.

As you learn to rest more easily in your true depth of being, spiritual profundity will replace sexual tension. An endless ease of being will grow more obvious even in the midst of passionate loving.

Unbound from chronic tension, your energy and consciousness are more available for continual practice. You are able to love all emotions that come and go, feeling through your kinks to your partner's heart more swiftly and consistently. Sex becomes an ongoing, conscious, whole-bodied participation in a profound ease and openness of being, in trusting communion with your lover, even while your body and emotions go through their twists and turns. Your practice thrives in the midst of tangles.

The glow of your sexual embers is no longer caught in the jumble of your kinks, but luxuriates brightly through them, a white-hot love without bounds. Your knots are made transparent, as are your edges. You and your lover are melded as one heart and then vanished to everywhere at light's speed.

Part Four:
Sexual Energy Exercises

Spontaneous openness and skillful practice go hand in hand to unfold joy in the way of enlightened sex. This section presents specific exercises to restore the natural flow of energy through the circuitry of your body so love can have its way. These exercises are universal in the sense that they have been discovered and rediscovered for thousands of years around the world, in China, Tibet, Japan, India, Europe, and the Americas. To make them effective, you must discover, and in every moment rediscover, these exercises for yourself. Practice them afresh, on the basis of your own revelation. Make these exercises your own.

The exercises work. But you have to *do* them, especially when your superficial habits of kink and closure attempt to reassert their hold on your deep loving. It's important to play with these exercises, sensitively fine-tuning them to untie your specific knots and unbind the natural flow of your sexual energy. For best results with all these exercises, combine stalwart self-discipline with moment-to-moment freshness, delight, and a large dollop of intuitive creativity.

While doing these exercises, remember this principle: The *power* of sexual energy flowing between lovers is usually determined by the feminine partner's openness to love and pleasure; the *depth* with which sexual energy flows between lovers is usually determined by the masculine partner's capacity to circulate energy consciously.

That is, sexual energy itself — its flavor, texture, and power — is a feminine gift. Where that sexual energy goes, or how it is used, is a masculine gift. Of course, we are each free to choose, moment by moment and year by year, when we might enjoy offering our more masculine or more feminine sexual gifts, regardless of whether we are man or woman, gay or straight.

If unbridled ecstasy can't fully express itself through the feminine partner's body, then sex will become cold, staid, and uninteresting. If the masculine partner is unable to move the couple to ever deeper revelations of love, surrender, and divine communion, then sex will become frustrating, amateurish, pathetic even, just a tease of its full potential.

Each of us has both masculine and feminine capacities within us. Therefore, each of us can *magnify* sexual energy (feminine) and *direct* sexual energy in specific ways (masculine). Yet, in any particular moment of sexual union, one person is usually playing the more feminine force of radiant power while the other is playing the more masculine force of present intentionality. One is being more attractive; one is being more directive. If this sexual polarity is denied or repressed — in either homosexual or heterosexual relationships — lovemaking tends to lose passion and depth.

When the exercises presented here get off the paper and into your bed, something curious may happen. As the sexual energy builds, the more feminine partner may forget to do the exercise you both set out to do. As love opens your hearts into ever widening joy and unbearable pleasure, the feminine partner often swoons in ecstasy too much to be concerned about some technical way to breathe or move energy.

Luckily, this works out fine because the masculine in each of us usually enjoys deepening and perfecting practices for growth.

During sex, if the masculine partner does an exercise deeply, with full presence, sensitivity, happiness, and skill, the feminine partner (if sufficiently open) will usually resonate quite effortlessly to the same depth. Sexually speaking, when partners respect, honor, and trust each other in love, the feminine flows where the masculine goes.

Therefore, if you are playing the feminine partner, don't worry if you become so blissfully open during sex that you don't remember to practice the technical breathing exercises that are presented here. Just relax into the natural pleasure of your body. Express your trust and pleasure to your partner when he is practicing well, and don't inhibit your expression of pain or boredom if he is not. Open to your own loving. Open to your partner's loving. Then open for the sake of love itself. Practice receiving love and energy into every part of your body, breath by breath. Surrender yourself utterly to be moved and breathed by love. Love will have its way.

These exercises may seem complicated at first, but they are simple once you've practiced them. As with learning to drive a car, at first you may feel overwhelmed by the details. How can you pay attention to the road in front of you while also checking your rearview mirror, knowing if the lanes are clear to your right and left, keeping an eye on your speedometer and gas gauge, figuring out when to accelerate, when to brake, and God forbid you should have to learn how to use a clutch and shift gears at the same time! But with a little practice, what first seems complicated becomes virtually effortless. And so it is with these sexual energy practices.

Practice as much of each exercise as you can remember, then review it again before your next opportunity to practice. Practice and review, practice and review. In time, you will be ready to expand beyond the fundamental practices described here because they will seem so easy — and so effortlessly blissful.

27. BREATHE SEXUAL ENERGY IN A CIRCLE

For many people, sex typically involves stimulating the genitals to experience pleasure. If this stimulated energy builds up beyond a certain point, most people can't contain it any more, so they release the energy in orgasm.

This is a very primitive and undeveloped form of sex, although it is the one with which most people are familiar. During this form of sex, it often feels as if the sexual energy wants to go down and be released outwardly. In most women, the energy accumulates and then is let go in waves, with the genitals and hips thrusting in fits of undulating release. In most men, sexual energy increases down in the genitals and then wants to be released outwardly in an ejaculative burst.

To move beyond this rudimentary heave of stimulation and release, you can learn to dissolve internal blocks, sustain much higher levels of pleasure than ever before, and circulate sexual energy in a way that gives the whole body an orgasm that fills, rather than depletes, your energy reserves. The first step in learning to do this involves allowing your internal sexual energy to circulate freely.

As described in Part One, when your natural internal circuitry is open, a main conduit of your energy moves in a circle, up the back of the body and down the front. During sex, your energy moves from the genitals back and then up the spine, fills the head, and then comes down the front of the body, through the tongue, throat, heart, solar plexus, and belly, back to the genital region, completing the circle.

In the practice of enlightened sex, you can learn to enjoy deeper genital orgasms, spine orgasms, brain orgasms, heart orgasms, and whole-body orgasms. You can magnify your internal energy to such an intensity that you are saturated by light far more blissful than any typical ejaculative or clitoral orgasm. You are able to surrender yourself fully through sex, to be obliterated in huge loving, for hours at a time, so your separateness is melted in the force of love that moves the universe. Sex becomes a means to help liberate the body and mind from limiting habits so you are able to open to your heart's most authentic and radiant truth, bursting to give your deepest gifts all day, at work, in relationships, and in meditation.

We will look at practices for circulating your sexual energy through your natural internal circuitry in stages.

It is fine to start off practicing these exercises while your partner is masturbating you or having genital intercourse with you, but it is often easier to learn to do the exercises while masturbating yourself. Eventually, you can practice these same exercises while making love with your partner.

First, practice to develop sensitivity to your internal energy itself, relaxing the body as much as possible. Tension in the body will decrease the flow of energy and mask the subtle currents of flow and movement that you need to feel in order to artfully circulate sexual energy. *Breathe full and deep.* As we will see, your breath can be used to help magnify and move energy. At the beginning, though, just practice keeping the breath full while you masturbate so you don't obstruct the energy in your body.

While masturbating, concentrate on feeling the energy as it builds up in your genital region. Where does this sexual energy come from? Where is this energy "stored"? Can you feel the texture of this energy and in which direction it is moving? Is it sharp, hot, cool, pulsating, or constant? Does it fill your abdomen, or just your genitals?

As you approach orgasm, you may feel the energy "trying" to flow out your genitals in an orgasmic spasm of release. Instead of allowing this pleasurable release of energy down and out your genital region, you will practice to reverse this flow, from your genitals back and up the spine. So, for now, do not masturbate to the point of orgasm.

Don't worry if you can't feel the subtleties of your internal sexual energy flow. Some people are more sensitive than others to the details of the flow of their internal energy. They are able to discriminate tingles from currents, upward from downward. Other people are only aware of being sexually turned on or turned off. With practice, everyone can become more sensitive to the flow of internal sexual energy. In the meantime, don't worry if you're not able to feel the subtle details of your internal energy flow—the exercises will still work.

28 BREATHE GENITAL ENERGY UP

While masturbating (or having sex with your partner), feel the energy build in the lower region of the body. When you feel a lot of sexual energy in the genital region, but still long before you would normally have an orgasm, contract your pelvic floor — including the genitals, perineum, and anus — and pull upward. (The perineum is the area between your anus and genitals.)

Tense or squeeze the muscles of the genitals, perineum, and anus as if you were trying to stop your urine flow. This upward contraction of your pelvic floor is known in yogic terms as *mula bandha*. In medical or therapeutic terms it is known by many names, including PC or Kegel exercises.

This contraction is not simply a squeeze but also involves an *upward tension* of the entire floor of the pelvis. If you are a man, this might feel like pulling your testicles up toward your body. If you are a woman, this might feel like squeezing an egg from the opening of your vagina up toward your cervix, or like an elevator moving up.

There are two basic ways to practice this upward contraction. One way is to contract the pelvic floor and hold the contraction for fifteen to thirty seconds while continuing to breathe normally. The other way is to contract and release the pelvic floor in rapid, rhythmic pulsations while breathing normally. Practicing both of these methods will help you train yourself quickly. You may practice for several minutes at a time, three or four times a day, as well as during sexual sessions. Rest if you feel tired. Don't overdo it.

During sexual stimulation, practice this upward pull of the pelvic floor—either as one long hold or as a cycle of quick contractions and releases—especially as your energy builds toward orgasm. Over time, as you develop sensitivity to the sexual energy flowing through your body, you can begin directing energy up your spine. For some people, this involves visualizing light or energy moving up the spine. Others feel the energy as a physical sensation, like heat, rushes of movement, a tingling thrill, or bubbles in champagne rising up the spine.

While you contract your pelvic floor, breathe through the nose as you feel the energy moving from your genitals backward and then up along your spine, rising with the gentle force of exhalation.

Sometimes practice *exhaling* up the spine. Other times practice *inhaling* up the spine. Become sensitive to what works best for you and when. At all times, though, your energy moves in a circle up your spine and down your front, regardless of how you coordinate this circulation with your breath.

With practice in breathing up the spine and contracting your pelvic floor just before you orgasm, you may be able to feel orgasm energy shooting up your spine and radiantly exploding through your head, rather than being released out your genitals. A brain orgasm that has risen through your whole body is much more pleasurable and rejuvenating than an orgasm that takes place solely in your genitals.

During a brain orgasm, it feels as if sexual energy rushes up your spine and explodes as light in the middle of your head. Then it pours down throughout your being as a healing rain of pervasive love. Sometimes during a brain orgasm, the energy will shoot out the top of your head, so you are light only, before descending back down into the body, saturating every cell with the vibrancy of bliss.

In addition to practicing the upward contraction of the pelvic floor while breathing up the spine during masturbation and sex, you can practice this exercise throughout the day to assist your natural energy flow, up your spine, through your head, and down your front in a circle. You can practice while walking down the street, while resting in bed, or while sitting at your office desk. Nobody needs to know.

29 BREATHE ENERGY DOWN THE FRONT

The natural and most healthy way for your internal energy to flow is in a circular path, up your spine and then down the front of your body. When this flow is reversed, you will feel energy moving up the front of your body. This reversed up-the-front flow of energy might manifest in many ways:

- When you become angry, your face may redden, your eyes may bulge out, and your head may feel like it is about to explode.

- At times you may become nervous and find yourself chatting away, seemingly unable to stop.

- On occasion you may become worried about something, mulling and cogitating, perhaps even unable to maintain an erection or become vaginally lubricated and relaxed.

- Energy flowing up your front may also manifest as digestive problems, tension in the jaw, and headaches.

When your energy flows in the natural way—down the front of your body—then your head relaxes and your belly and genital region fill with energy, increasing your sexual vitality and strengthening your personal power throughout the day. Your personal power is your capacity to act creatively, in spite of the challenges that may face you in life and relationship. True personal power is the force of love. It is your capacity to bring love into a world or relationship that may be characterized in the moment by fear or resistance.

To enlarge your sexual capacity and personal power, practice drawing energy down the front of your body throughout the day, while sitting, standing, walking, or lying down. It is often easiest to begin this practice while lying on your back with your hands resting on your belly, your knees bent, and your feet flat on the floor.

For most people, it is best to draw energy down the front of the body while *inhaling* through the nose. (You may want to experiment by drawing energy down your front while *exhaling* in order to determine which way works best for you.) *While inhaling, feel as if energy is being drawn down the front of your body, from the top of your head down into your belly and genitals.* Your belly can expand with every inhale, as if you are becoming pregnant with energy. Then your belly can contract gently inward as you exhale energy up your spine.

Unless otherwise indicated, keep your mouth closed and the tip of your tongue pressed gently against the roof of your mouth as you inhale and exhale through your nose. Your tongue provides a bridge across which energy can flow from your head down through the front of your body: throat, heart, solar plexus, belly, and genitals.

As your belly expands and you inhale energy down the front of your body, feel as if your genitals and lower abdomen receive and accumulate energy. It is as if you are recharging a battery in your lower body. Eventually, after several weeks of practice, you may be able to arouse your genitals or revitalize your personal power simply by consciously inhaling energy fully down the front of your body.

You can also help your partner strengthen his or her practice of inhaling energy down the front of the body. *Start with your partner lying on his or her back with knees bent and feet flat on the floor. Put your hand on your partner's belly just below the navel so that your palm is flat against the flesh. By vibrating your hand slightly or moving it in a circular motion on the lower belly, help your partner soften and relax the belly. Then, with your hand still gently massaging or vibrating your partner's belly, guide him or her to inhale and draw breath and energy down the front and into the belly.* As your partner inhales, the belly should fill with breath and your hand should rise as the belly becomes pregnant with energy, full, and round.

If you both feel it is appropriate, you can move your hand from the belly to your lover's genitals. Your gentle touch on your lover's genitals may help your lover remember to draw inhaled breath energy down his or her front, through the lower abdomen, all the way to the genitals and pelvic floor.

Another good way to assist your partner in learning to move energy down the front is by using your hands to stroke down the front of your partner's body from the heart to the lower belly, during sex or at any time. You can use this technique if your partner's face is getting red with the heat of anger or passion rising the "wrong way," up the front of the body toward the head. You can bring this hot energy quickly into proper downward circulation by lovingly stroking down the front of your partner's body, as if coaxing the energy to move down the front, like a waterfall of molten lava, rather than up the front, like a hot geyser.

Over time, as you practice breathing energy down the front, you will become aware of a growing center of power residing in your lower belly. As you accumulate energy in your belly through proper breathing, you will be able to meet the obstructions in your daily life with greater energy, and give your gift with gentle but persistent force, humor, and emotional perseverance. You will be able to transmit healing energy by directing it through your heart, hands, eyes, and genitals. You will be able to embrace your lover with tremendous sexual potency, softness, stamina, and loving surrender.

As paradoxical as it might sound, most people need to strengthen their bodies before they will surrender fully. Once your personal power is strengthened and your belly is full of life force, you can relax physically and emotionally without fear. You can let down the defenses around your heart, certain that your surrender and opening is based on strength rather than weakness.

As your personal power grows, you begin to realize a continuity of energy: the life force you are breathing through your body is the same unlimited life force flowing all around you and also through your partner. By surrendering, by opening to love and magnifying the flow of energy in sexual embrace, you open directly to a boundless and universal flow of energy that circulates throughout your body.

True surrender is true power: the love-force that moves the universe is also the love-force that breathes your breath and beats your heart. When fear dissolves, you no longer separate yourself from this single flow of immense force. Love is continuity with infinite life force, a oneness of being with no separation. Opening sexually is opening to this flow of life force. And love is the key to this opening. But before you can trust love, you need to be strong enough to relax.

Besides increasing sexual energy and personal power—thus enabling you to surrender in love more deeply—breathing energy down the front of your body brings equilibrium to agitated thoughts and emotions. Your face, jaw, heart, and belly open and relax in the natural downward flow of energy. Unnecessary chatter slows down, anger is cooled, and tension is eased. When you practice opening the entire circuit of internal energy, breathing energy up the spine and down the front, you will naturally create a proper balance for a life of vitality and relaxation, incarnated love and transcendental bliss, both sexually and in everyday life.

30 SEAL YOUR PELVIC FLOOR

The natural circuit of sexual energy flows from your genitals up your spine and into or through your head, then back down the front of your body, down to your pelvic floor. During sex and throughout the day, you can learn to seal the entire pelvic floor—including the genitals, perineum, and anus—so your magnified energy doesn't leak out at the base.

Sealing your pelvic floor and drawing the stimulated sexual energy up your spine at first requires an upward muscular contraction of the anus, perineum, and genitals, as already described. Eventually, the buttocks and anus remain more relaxed, and only a slight upward tension is applied in the genital and perineal region. Over time, even this slight upward pull becomes more and more subtle, evolving into a practice of conscious intention—merely feeling and intending the energy to move up the spine from the genitals—rather than a physical exercise of muscular contraction. Finally, these practices occur spontaneously.

As you begin to practice, the upward contraction of your pelvic floor helps to contain your energy within the natural circuitry of your body so that it flows up your spine and down your front, during sex and throughout the day. As your practice deepens and your sensitivity increases, you will naturally discover other ways to make conscious use of your pelvic floor:

1. *Learn to bounce energy off your pelvic floor.* This practice can be done while masturbating, while having sex with your partner, or at any time during the day. Inhale deeply down the front of your body for several cycles of breath (each cycle consists of an

inhale and an exhale), feeling energy accumulate in your lower abdomen and genital region.

When the energy in your lower belly feels full, draw it forcefully down to your pelvic floor with an inhalation, and then with an equally strong exhalation and contraction of the pelvic floor, bounce the energy up your spine. The contraction of your pelvic floor moves your energy upward as if your energy were bouncing off a trampoline.

At first, you should feel a movement of energy up your spine and perhaps a pleasant sensation of gentle pressure in your head. Eventually the upwardly shooting energy may explode in colors inside your head, or it may even shoot out the top of your head in a rise of bliss before descending into your body as a sublime pressure of love. During these practices, your head may open and feel as if it's turned inside out. Simply relax, breathe fully, and offer love through your entire body, even during unusual experiences such as this.

2. *When you are proficient at moving energy in your own body, practice bouncing energy from your pelvic floor up your partner's spine.* While having sex, draw several slow and full inhalations down the front of your body to accumulate energy in your lower belly and genital region. Then, with a strong exhalation, contract your pelvic floor and, with intention and visualization, bounce the energy through your genitals upward through *your partner's* spine. *After the energy shoots up your partner's spine, remember to inhale the descending energy back down your partner's front.* In this way, you complete the entire circle of energy in your partner's body.

You may do this exercise by *visualizing* the energy moving from your own genital region up your partner's spine. Or perhaps you will actually *feel* the energy moving down your own front, bouncing off your pelvic floor, and up through your partner. For now, while you become more sensitive to the flow of internal energy, simply *intend* the energy to move up your partner's spine, in coordination with your breath and the trampoline-like contraction of your pelvic floor.

This practice can be engaged while having sex or while embracing your partner fully clothed. At first, your partner may not feel much of your energy. But as the strength of your capacity to transmit energy increases, your partner will be able to feel the ascending energy very strongly. Your partner may swoon in this upward flow of energy, closing his or her eyes, making sounds of bliss, and even experiencing orgasms in the genitals, heart, and head—whether or not you are actually having sex. It all depends on the strength of your energy transmission and your partner's capacity to receive energy. Practice with patience, as it may take months (or weeks or hours) to develop sufficient proficiency.

At first, either you or your partner should practice this exercise while the other receives the results. *Eventually, you and your partner may choose to practice this exercise by simultaneously breathing energy up each other's spine and breathing energy down each other's front.* This simultaneous practice is particularly effective at loosening deep energetic blocks and restoring natural ease and full flow to the entire circuit of your internal life force.

3. During the day, notice if your pelvic floor feels "open," as if energy were leaking out. *If your pelvic floor feels leaky, seal the energetic seepage with several strong contractions.* For instance, right after you urinate or move your bowels, your genital region or anus may still feel opened or uncontained. If so, after using the toilet, perform several strong upward contractions of your pelvic floor. Inhale fully, contract your pelvic floor, hold your breath for a moment, release the contraction, and then exhale. Eventually, you

may want to hold the contraction steady through several cycles of inhalation and exhalation before relaxing.

4. *If you begin to feel tired during the day, you can energize your body by inhaling and bringing energy to your belly, to your genital region, and down to your pelvic floor with several full inhalations. Then you can expand that energy upward throughout your body by contracting your pelvic floor and bouncing the energy upward with an exhalation.* (Again, after experimentation, some people may find that it works better for them to bounce energy up the spine with an inhalation and bring energy down the front with an exhalation.)

5. You can give a person energy from a distance for the sake of healing or revitalization without any physical contact at all. *Over the course of several full inhalations down your front, accumulate energy in your abdomen and genital region. Then bounce it to the person with an upward contraction of your pelvic floor combined with exhalation, visualization, and feeling-intention.* That is, along with the physical part of the exercise, lovingly intend your energy toward the person to whom you would like to give it. Feel the energy filling the person with healing and light. Once you learn how to accumulate and move energy, you will be surprised at the results. Although this kind of exercise may seem like wishful thinking at first, with practice, the transmission of energy becomes very powerful, effective, and tangible both to you and to others.

31 LOCK ENERGY IN YOUR SOFT PARTS

The "soft parts" of your body are the most important places through which to regulate the flow of internal sexual energy. In addition to your anus, genitals, and perineum, the soft parts include your throat and entire belly area.

Throat Area

As mentioned earlier, during sex it is important to keep the tip of your tongue gently pressed against the roof of your mouth in order to complete your internal circuit so energy can flow from your head down through the front of your body. In addition, the tongue can also be used to regulate a "diaphragm" located near the back of the throat. *With some strength, push the thick back part of your tongue up into the soft palate toward the rear of the roof of your mouth while you contract your upper throat.* If you do this exercise correctly, you will feel a pressure in your head.

By experimenting during your sexual practice, you can determine just the right moments to apply this tongue pressure to help move the flow of energy upward and temporarily seal energy in the head (for example, during brain orgasms). *After applying this energy lock, always remember to draw the energy back down the front of the body with a full inhalation and an expanding belly so the energy doesn't become stuck in the head area and create pain or tension.*

Belly Area

The solar plexus—the soft region in the center of the body, just below the ribs and above the navel—is another major energy regulator. The solar plexus should, in general, remain completely relaxed. If energy is flowing unobstructed through your complete internal circuit during sex, you will experience a pleasant sensation of fullness in the solar plexus, as well as the whole abdominal region, as this entire area fills with sexual energy descending down your front.

Occasionally, you may want to emphasize the upward flow of energy along your spine, perhaps when you have accumulated too much energy in your genitals or when you want to experience a whole-body or brain orgasm rather than a genital orgasm. We have already described how to do this by using your breath, intention, visualization, and upward tension in your pelvic floor. The solar plexus and the entire belly can participate in this process, especially when the urge toward genital orgasm becomes particularly intense. We will look at two basic methods for contracting the belly and solar plexus.

The first method increases the upward flow of energy so that it fills the body. *Inhale energy up the spine while simultaneously contracting and pulling in your pelvic floor, belly, and solar plexus. Your belly and solar plexus move in toward the spine as you inhale (the opposite of their normal movement), then lift up toward the head.*

Your belly and solar plexus are not merely made hard and tense, but are actually made hollow or concave as you inhale, pulling inward and "scooping" upward during the contraction. Remember that normally your belly and solar plexus expand with your inhale, as energy moves down and fills the front of the body. This exercise of pulling inward and upward with your inhale is a unique practice for helping to convert genital orgasms into whole-body orgasms.

A second method can also be used for equilibrating genital energy and continuing to make love without an excessive urge toward ejaculative or depleting orgasm. First, exhale all your breath. It is important to exhale completely, so you feel no air remaining in the body at all. Then, while you are still empty of air, simultaneously contract your pelvic floor, belly, and solar plexus while pulling inward and upward at all these areas.

In other words, after a complete exhalation, hold the breath out of your body while applying inward and upward tension at the front of your body all the way from your anus to your ribs. Your belly is sucked inward—the entire area from your pubic bone to your sternum is concave. Hold this for as long as you comfortably can, while your breath remains held out. (For added effect, you may also apply the tongue pressure toward the back of the throat that we discussed previously.)

When you finally need to inhale, first relax the front of your body and then inhale slowly and deeply, allowing your belly and solar plexus to become large, soft, and round. It is good to maintain a subtle upward tension of the pelvic floor in order to seal the energy that comes down the front with your inhale.

While you are holding the exhaled breath out and your belly and solar plexus are contracted inward and upward, energy in your lower body will dissipate upward. Your excess genital stimulation will spread out as the energy moves upward throughout your body.

Follow this exercise with several cycles of full and deep breathing down the front and up the spine, circulating fresh energy in a smooth and even fashion. The intensity of your genital energy will spread wide, easing into a whole-body fullness and internal brightness.

All these exercises are best learned by making them quite muscular at first. While doing the throat lock, for instance, really push the broad part of the back of your tongue up toward the back of your throat. While doing the abdominal lock, really pull the belly and solar plexus inward and upward with significant force and strength. This takes practice, but over time it will become easy and effortless. You can feel the effects of these exercises on your energy immediately, and you will begin to develop a style that works best for you.

Once you know how to do the basic exercises with good results, you can experiment with making the motions more and more subtle. *Over time, the muscular contractions will become less and less outwardly obvious, as you are able to simply intend the energy to move in different ways through your body.* You will be able to feel and direct your internal energy, as well as the energy of your partner, by using subtle internal adjustments and eventually by means of simple feeling, breath, and intention. The muscularity of the exercises will decrease as you become more sensitive to the internal circuitry of your body and more adept at regulating the flow of sexual energy in your body.

Eventually, it becomes just as easy to regulate the energy flow in your partner's body as in yours. Then, with your intentions unified, you can heal one another through the mutual flow of energy, resting more deeply in the ongoing and effortless beauty of conscious love and radiant openness. With practice, sex becomes a full merger in the motionless peal of light, as all the channels in your body and your partner's body are opened and summarized as a single force of love.

CONCLUSION

Enlightened sex is rare. Even after learning how to make love, we will often refuse. We may blame our partner for not loving us, for betraying, rejecting, or ignoring us. We may blame our body for being too tired and the world for being too difficult and painful. We may blame the universe for denying us the right lover—or maybe our family and professional life require too much for us to surrender in the bloom of unbearable pleasure. We long for the same fullness of bliss that we never seem to have time to offer. We complain about our life and blame others, until we realize that right now, we *are* making love. Or we are *refusing*—right now.

No blame is necessary; no blame is useful. We are either offering love or refusing to do so.

Imagine you are with your lover, who is closed down and not willing to connect with you. First, feel your lover. Be willing to feel your lover more than you feel yourself. Feel your lover's rhythm of breathing, as well as his or her tension, posture, and mood. Look at your lover's face, and feel the history creased into his or her skin. Be willing to feel your lover's joy and sorrow, anguish and anger. Your lover feels alone much of the time, and yearns for more and truer love, just as you do. Your lover, too, often experiences himself or herself as separate and emotionally isolated, and blames others—perhaps you—for not loving him or her enough. Your lover can feel as trapped by life and abandoned by love as you do.

Whether it is you or your lover who seems closed down, your responsibility as a superior lover is to offer love. If your body is tense, then do your best to relax and offer love through your body. If your breath is tight, do your best to breathe deeply and easefully, offering love by connecting your breath with your partner's. If you are occupied by your own emotions and thoughts, feel beyond yourself so you can fully feel your lover. Feeling fully is love.

Enlightened sex means to feel beyond your own body, mind, and emotions so you can feel your lover's. Then, feel even beyond your lover. Include yourself and your lover, but also feel outward to the horizons of every present moment. While making love, feel everything. Help your lover to open and feel by offering your own open feeling as a gift.

Enlightened sex means unlimited feeling. If we collapse our feeling onto ourselves, limiting our feeling to our own body, mind, and emotions, then we are not practicing enlightened sex.

When you have felt your lover's heart and body and breath, gaze deep into his or her eyes, which are portals to the soul. Sustain your eyes, body, and breath wide open. Even if your lover refuses, sustain openness. Your heart will want to close down to protect itself from the insult of your lover's rejection, but a protected heart is unable to feel. A protected heart is a limit on love. Unguard your heart over and over in the face of your lover's closure, rejection, and betrayal.

Like a reflex, your heart will close to protect itself when your lover pulls away or closes down. Practice to open and feel, even when your lover hurts your heart. In many short moments repeated frequently, reopen and re-feel your lover, and also feel beyond your lover. Actually feel your lover, then feel the space around your lover, and feel outward to the furthest reaches of feeling. This is how to train in enlightened sex. Over and over, notice you are refusing to love fully, then consent to love.

Notice you are holding back your feelers, then allow your feeling to enter deep into your lover's heart and to spread wide to feel all beings. Be willing to suffer your partner's and everybody's closure without closing yourself. And if you do close, remember to open again. Continually re-offer the opportunity for you and your partner to open together in love and feel all.

This choice to open and feel is our fundamental moment-by-moment practice in enlightened sex. Instead of focusing merely on our own pleasure, or reacting to our partner's coming and going, we train to feel through and beyond every experience. We don't avoid our own sensations and emotions or those of our lover. We feel them, but we don't stop there, perpetually fixated on thoughts and emotions. With training, our hearts become spacious, allowing room for embracing and making love with all thoughts and emotions, pleasures and pains, as they come and go. Even when our partner betrays us, we remember to open and feel, over and over. We may choose to change our behaviors — or our relationships — but such choices emerge from an open, feeling heart.

Light flows from our open heart. Our face becomes radiant with the flush of love. Our sexing becomes a dance of delight. Should we stub our toe, we may say, "Ouch!" And then we re-open and connect with our partner, feeling outward as love, again and again. This is enlightened sex, and the skills presented in this manual for being a superior lover are steps to help us learn the basic moves and rhythms so that the light of love may shine through our passion.

May our sex always flower as an offering of love's light.

ABOUT SOUNDS TRUE

Sounds True was founded in 1985 with a clear vision: to disseminate spiritual wisdom. Located in Boulder, Colorado, Sounds True publishes teaching programs that are designed to educate, uplift, and inspire. We work with many of the leading spiritual teachers, thinkers, healers, and visionary artists of our time.

To receive a free catalog of tools and teachings for personal and spiritual transformation, please visit www.soundstrue.com, call toll-free 800-333-9185, or write to us at the address below.

Sounds True
PO Box 8010
Boulder CO 80306

DAVID DEIDA RESOURCES

BOOKS

The Way of the Superior Man
A Spiritual Guide to Mastering the Challenges of Women, Work, and Sexual Desire
David Deida explores the most important issues in men's lives — from career and family to women and intimacy to love and sex — to offer the ultimate spiritual guide for men living a life of integrity, authenticity, and freedom.
ISBN: 978-1-59179-257-4 / U.S. $17.95

Dear Lover
A Woman's Guide to Men, Sex, and Love's Deepest Bliss
How do you attract and keep a man capable of meeting what you most passionately yearn for? To answer this question, David Deida explores every aspect of the feminine practice of spiritual intimacy, from sexuality and lovemaking to family and career to emotions, trust, and commitment.
ISBN: 978-1-59179-260-4 / U.S. $16.95

Blue Truth
A Spiritual Guide to Life & Death and Love & Sex
David Deida presents a treasury of skills
and insights for uncovering and offering
your true heart of purpose, passion, and
unquenchable love.
ISBN: 978-1-59179-259-8 / U.S. $16.95

Finding God Through Sex
Awakening the One of Spirit
Through the Two of Flesh
No matter how much we pray or meditate,
it's not always easy to integrate sexual pleasure
and spiritual depth. David Deida helps single
men and women and couples of every orientation turn sex into
an erotic act of deep devotional surrender.
ISBN: 978-1-59179-273-4 / U.S $16.95

Wild Nights
Conversations with Mykonos about Passionate
Love, Extraordinary Sex, and How to Open to God
Meet Mykonos—scurrilous madman,
and speaker of truth. A recollection of a
unique relationship between a student and an extraordinary
spiritual teacher.
ISBN: 978-1-59179-233-8 / U.S. $15.95

Instant Enlightenment

Fast, Deep, and Sexy

David Deida offers a wealth of priceless exercises and insights to bring "instant enlightenment" to the areas we need it most.

ISBN: 978-1-59179-560-5 / U.S. $12.95

Also Available

Intimate Communion

Awakening Your Sexual Essence

David Deida's first book lays the foundation for his teaching on the integration of intimacy and authentic spiritual practice.

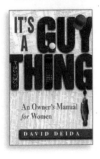

It's a Guy Thing

An Owner's Manual for Women

David Deida answers over 150 of women's most asked questions about men and intimacy.

AUDIO

Enlightened Sex
Finding Freedom & Fullness Through Sexual Union
A complete six-CD program to learn the secrets
to transforming lovemaking into a spiritual gift
to yourself, your lover, and the world.

ISBN: 978-1-59179-083-9 / U.S. $69.95

The Teaching Sessions:
The Way of the Superior Man
*Revolutionary Tools and Essential Exercises
for Mastering the Challenges of Women, Work,
and Sexual Desire*

A spiritual guide for today's man in search of the secrets to
success in career, purpose, and sexual intimacy — now available
on four CDs in this original author expansion of and companion
to the bestselling book.

ISBN: 978-1-59179-343-4 / U.S. $29.95

For information about all of David Deida's books and audio,
visit **www.deida.info**.

To place an order or to receive a free catalog of wisdom teachings
for the inner life, visit **www.soundstrue.com**, call toll-free
800-333-9185, or write: The Sounds True Catalog, PO Box 8010,
Boulder CO 80306.

ABOUT THE AUTHOR

Acknowledged as one of the most insightful and provocative teachers of our time, bestselling author David Deida continues to revolutionize the way that men and women grow spiritually and sexually. His books have been published in more than twenty languages. His workshops on a radically practical spirituality have been hailed as among the most original and authentic contributions to the field of self-development currently available.

For more information about David Deida's books, audio, video, and teaching schedule, please go to **www.deida.info.**